PRAISE FOR

CurBCheK
R E L O A D

"If you like no nonsense, cut to the chase monologs, this is for you. I couldn't help but flash back to the old 1960s TV show as I read this book. Anyone who enjoys their police stories to be hard hitting and factual will really enjoy this."
• Jeannie Walker—Award Winning Author of "Fighting the Devil" •

"Following the already dark and gritty 2011 release of *CurbChek, CurbChek Reload* ramps everything up a level, the cops, the criminals, the anger and frustration...everything that made the first book interesting, albeit disturbing and heartbreaking, is back but with a vengeance!"
• Nylon Admiral •

"This is a really good book, which tells how things are out there at night in the ghettos of America, where hope has left the building. I say buy this book. It is a page turner—no kidding. This guy can write."
• Rip Kitty •

"You haven't seen anything until you have read *CurbChek Reload*. Fortier takes you on a ride with him at many of his most difficult, violent, heart wrenching, and disturbing calls. Do I want to go on a ride-along? Not a chance...and especially not with Zach. This was a great read!"
• J. Pearson •

"These are gritty, honest, no-holds-barred glimpses into the life of a street cop. Told in the language we (cops and ex cops) use—no BS, no sugar coating, no avoiding the hard topics, and always with a dose of very dark humor for the most inappropriate things. Highly recommended!"
• Holly Cochran •

CURBCHEK

RELOAD

ZACH FORTIER

steeleshark
press

Cover design, interior book design
and eBook design
by Blue Harvest Creative
www.blueharvestcreative.com

CURBCHEK RELOAD

Copyright © 2012, 2013 Zach Fortier

Published by
SteeleShark Press

ISBN-13: 978-0615880167
ISBN-10: 0615880169

Visit the author at:
Website: *www.curbchek.com*
Blog: *www.authorzachfortier.blogspot.com*
Facebook: *www.facebook.com/authorzach.fortier*
Twitter: *www.twitter.com/zachfortier1*
Goodreads: *www.goodreads.com/author/show/5164780.Zach_Fortier*

ALSO BY ZACH FORTIER

CurbChek

Street Creds

Hero to Zero

1
We Were Made For Each Other

PEOPLE TALK A LOT OF trash about cops and all night donut shops and 24-hour convenience stores. I've heard it my whole career: if you want a cop, go to the nearest 7-11 or donut shop, and there they'll be. There's a reason for that; several, actually. Midnight shift is long, and you get tired. The more fatigued you are, the more you crave sweets.

I ate an amazing amount of gum and candy bars. They'd keep me awake and somewhat sharp after the rush of calls had ended at about 4:30 a.m. and we were left with the early risers, Daywalkers beginning to exit their homes and retake the city.

Some cops ate donuts, some candy, some fruit, but we all craved sweets to fight the fatigue. We all had a store that we staked out as ours. Sometimes it was that the coffee was better at that store or the clerk was someone you could talk to that wouldn't ask stupid questions. But we all took a store as ours to protect and watch over.

That, too, was the reality. We were there to keep them safe. Shit could break loose at an all-night store fast. The clerks weren't able to defend themselves against the predators of the night. You never knew what would walk through the door, or when, if you were a clerk at one of the stores.

The clerks often offered free food or coffee if we'd hang out at the store. Sometimes guys abused the offers, and sometimes they didn't.

The clerks were a wealth of information as to what was going on in my area. They could tell you the latest drug trends or who the newest hookers were in the area, and I'd frequently ask them questions, picking their brains about what was going on.

People came into the store all night, talking trash, drunk, high, and completely unaware of the information they spilled in front of the anonymous clerks. I took their input into my area's trends very seriously.

Train the clerk to watch out for who you were looking for—or better yet, find a clerk that was already aware of the street—and you had a relationship that would benefit you both.

I learned a lot from the clerks. One guy explained to me why they were always out of the antifreeze testers. He said that they ordered them in by the hundreds and they'd be sold out in hours. I had no idea they went through so many.

He said that the testers were made of tempered glass, able to withstand heat. Crackheads and tweekers would buy them and empty the glass tubes, modifying them into glass pipes to smoke their drug of choice. (Street people referred to them as the "glass dick" and said that tweekers and crackheads were slaves to the "glass dick", referring to a look of relief and enjoyment that porn stars, crackheads and tweekers all shared during their oral relief).

I was amazed. I knew that they used the glass pipes, but I had no idea where they got them. Any automotive shop or 7-11 carried the testers, and they were always running out of them in my area. The clerks taught me a lot, upping my street IQ. I was always happy to learn from anyone who would teach me.

One night, we came out of briefing and hit the ground running. The calls were stacked up, and none were small or minor. The city was rocking, and we had to step it up to meet the challenge. We couldn't gradually step into the street tonight. It would be a strange night.

Normally, we all met at an all-night convenience store and hung with Sergeant Duke. He was one of the few sergeants we all liked. He was one of us, and not admin. He took a special pride in his squad and made us feel like what we each did mattered.

This was a direct contrast to the Chief, who repeatedly told us we could be replaced by anyone and at anytime. He admitted to us that he was a "bean counter", and it showed in his management philosophy. We, too, were nothing but beans to be counted, and nothing we did mattered or was special. The man was an idiot.

Anyway, this night we couldn't meet at the store for our regular bullshit session before we hit the streets. It was a case of fate, and I wonder how things would have turned out if it had been slow that night instead of so frantic.

Meanwhile, the clerk wondered where we were. She had the coffee ready, freshly brewed. Minutes ticked past, and still we didn't show. We were so busy, I wouldn't hear about the incident that was about to occur 'til the next day.

Some nights, it seemed to us that the city was infected with an evil disease, like on one of the popular zombie movies.

The city was alive with crimes in progress; shootings and stabbings. You could hear the sirens screaming and the patrol cars' motors gearing up as we bounced from call to call, putting out fires and keeping the dark side of the population in check.

Tom Miller was a frequent client of the store, and we saw him nearly every night we were there. He was on Social Security and lived on a small amount of money in an apartment near the store.

He was one of the night people that Daywalkers are barely aware of. He was mentally disabled, but he appeared to us to be harmless. He'd often stop and talk to us as he stopped in on his nightly quest for a large Mountain Dew and candy. He never said one hostile word to us or to the clerk. We were aware of him, but he wasn't perceived by any of us as a threat.

What we didn't know was he was schizophrenic. As long as he was on his medication, he did really well; but for some reason, the voices got to him one day. They were a little louder.

Maybe he forgot to take his medication, or maybe he needed the dosage to be increased; I don't know.

He started to hear the voices again, and they told him to quit taking his medication. He did quit taking his medication, and the downhill spiral was rapid after that. He became worse and more paranoid. He quit coming to the store at night and stayed in his apartment.

The night we were running throughout the city, trying to keep the chaos from getting out of hand, he was at his worst. The voices had spoken to him for days, telling him to go to the store and kill us all.

He had a shotgun, and he loaded it up and waited for the time we normally showed up at the store. He left his apartment, walking the two or three blocks to the store then walked in, shotgun loaded, finger on the trigger, safety off, ready to go.

We weren't there. The clerk saw him and immediately dialed 911. He walked through the store, looking for us—but saw no one. He went to the clerk, who was on the phone, and started shooting.

He had no intention of robbing her or us. The voices were clear: kill them all! He shot the woman at point blank range, blowing her shoulder and left arm completely off. He reloaded and shot her again, then set the weapon down on the counter and waited for the cops to come.

Who knows what would have happened if we had been there? Maybe he would have killed a couple of us, maybe not. Maybe we would have killed him and the clerk wouldn't have been harmed.

The "what if" shit drove us crazy. We felt responsible for her injuries, feeling guilty for not being there when she needed us. We had a relationship with her as a squad. We took care of each other.

Again, there was a feeling that we'd failed. You couldn't be there every time, every place, everywhere you were needed. No matter how you tried, no matter how much you educated yourself in the ways of the streets, there was always random shit like this that was brutal and life altering.

We tried to go back to the store, but the guilt was too much. Our bullshit sessions were over, and no one said a word, but we all felt like we'd failed her.

The clerk somehow survived, but she'd be forever handicapped by the shooting. We started to meet at other stores and in smaller groups. We couldn't face the feelings of failure that being in that store brought us.

We failed all night long every night to win back the streets. As hard as we tried, we barely kept the shit in check. We had to have someplace to go and feel that we didn't fail, even if it was an illusion.

Hero To Zero:
A Rude Awakening

ONE SATURDAY, WHILE WAITING IN line to go to lunch behind the list of other officers that had beat me to the punch and got on the lunch list, I was dispatched to an unknown 911 call at a facility that took care of severely handicapped patients.

The caller had whispered to come quick, that he was being beaten by the caregivers, and then he hung up.

Dispatch had called back and reached a caregiver in the home, a male adult. He said that one of the patients had been able to get a hold of the cordless phone and made the call. He said the patient did not want to be there but that he was all right and no police response was needed.

I went anyway. Calls like this never happened; not once had I been to a nursing home or care facility for a 911 call, so I was suspicious. The dispatcher agreed, saying the whispering voice sounded sincerely afraid and could possibly have been crying.

I arrived at the facility and located the caregiver. He was a huge man and I later found out he was a college football player, one of the defensive linemen. He had taken this job because it was easy and fit into his class schedule; he could study at night and get paid for it while he was at work.

The college had arranged for the player to get the job as part of his "agreement" to play for the school.

Anyway, this dude was a mountain, 6'5", well over 300 pounds, and solid. I was talking to him, and he seemed fairly at ease. I asked to look around, and he said, "Sure, go ahead."

Nothing seemed out of the ordinary, so I asked which one of the patients had called. He told me that a middle aged man who was in a wheelchair had called. He called him Mr. Robins. I asked to speak to Mr. Robins alone, and again the Mountain agreed and let me have the room to speak in private.

Mr. Robins was confined to a wheelchair. He had a neurological disorder that had left him crippled and barely able to move the chair. He had these really thick glasses, and his eyes were huge behind them while we talked.

I asked him if he had called, and if so, why? He asked me if the Mountain had left the room, and I said that yes, he had. Mr. Robins started to cry and detailed to me that the Mountain had abused him for months. He said that the Mountain had repeatedly degraded and humiliated him, calling him "cripple" and "vegetable man", and sometimes referring to him as "V-8" for the vegetable drink.

He had tried to ignore the abuse and said that eventually, when he did not react, the Mountain had started to punch him. He said the mountain never punched him when anyone else was in the room.

He was sobbing as he told me this. He said the Mountain would pick him up by the shoulders, completely out of the wheelchair, then shake him and threaten to throw him against the wall.

He was hysterical while telling me his story. I asked him if he had any marks or bruises that he could show me to help support this claim.

He said, "Oh, hell yes!"

Mr. Robins had me unbutton his shirt and pull his arm out of the sleeve. Obvious deep bruises covered his arm and chest; in my mind, there was no doubt that he was being abused.

I told him not to worry, that the abuse would end today; I would make sure of it.

I called for another unit to assist me on the call.

While I waited, Mr. Robins told me that the Mountain was only one of several caregivers that abused him in the facility and that he would have to be removed from the facility to be truly safe.

He said, "I beg you, please don't leave me here; there is no way I will survive the night if you do."

When the other unit arrived, I left Mr. Robins and began to question the Mountain. He readily admitted abusing the wheelchair-bound man, stating that he was a piece of shit and sometimes just needed his ass kicked back into line. After he had been slapped around a bit, he was less mouthy and did what he was told.

The Mountain said that he never really hit the man too hard; just enough to scare him and intimidate him into compliance—that way, he could get back to studying.

The Mountain made a point of telling me that he was protected by the college and that that they would back him up on his statement. He was one of the stars of the football team, and they needed him to win; that was his twisted logic.

This kind of arrogance is not that rare. Everyone believes that they are exempt from the law for one reason or another. Everyone thinks that they are special, that they can speed through school zones, smoke meth, drive drunk, beat their spouse—whatever they wish—and when we show up, they respond just like the Mountain.

When I told him he was under arrest for abusing a disabled person and that there was an enhancement because he was a person of trust, he came unglued. He stated the same old standby you hear over and over again: "Why don't you go out and arrest some real criminals and leave me alone?"

The Mountain went down without a fight. The back up unit took him to jail for me while I worked on finding the manager of the facility.

I couldn't locate anyone, so I left messages and called the state agency that was responsible for licensing the home; I was going to make sure this abuse was stopped today.

I called CSI and had pictures taken of Mr. Robins' injuries, advised the Sergeant of what had happened, then called DFS (Division of Family Services) to get Mr. Robins temporarily placed in another home.

I had a worker on the way to pick him up and was feeling pretty good about the work I had done. The bad guy was locked up, and the helpless victim was free from continued abuse. The bruises were real and serious.

The Sergeant told me I had done a great job and to let him know when it was all cleaned up—then the phone rang; it was the facility's director.

I told the director what had happened, and at first he was in disbelief. I told him that I had personally seen the injuries to Mr. Robins and that the Mountain had admitted to me that he had slapped Mr. Robins around, 'but only when he needed it.'

The director was very upset about this, saying that this was horrible and that he would be right in. I told him that would be fine but that I had called DFS and that Mr. Robins would be removed from the facility that night for his protection.

The director became really quiet and then said, "Officer, you need to listen to me very carefully: do not remove Mr. Robins from that facility under any circumstances."

I told him that I had no choice. Mr. Robins was in danger, and I had to ensure his safety before I left. He said, "Mr. Robins is not what he appears to be; he is a very dangerous man. Do not take him out of that facility."

I turned and looked at the wheelchair-bound man, noticeably relieved that he was safe from further abuse.

I then said, "How in the hell is he dangerous? He is helpless!"

The director told me that Mr. Robins was a violent pedophile that preferred to abuse infants. He had been arrested and convicted for nearly killing two infants that he had raped.

He had played the helpless invalid in his family and had gained the trust of one of the family members. He then took advantage of a moment where he had been left alone in a room with two infants and had brutally raped both of them, causing severe internal damage to the babies.

I looked at the handicapped, meek Mr. Robins and thought no way this could be true.

I told the director I would wait for his arrival and that he needed to be prepared to show me the court documents placing Mr. Robins in the home. Meanwhile, I called our records division and had them run Mr. Robins.

While they checked him out, I knelt down and quietly asked him about the allegations. He said nothing for several seconds, then responded. It was like a switch had been thrown in his mind: the meek and mild Mr. Robins was gone; suddenly, he was like a rabid dog, spouting, "Fuck you!" and "I was almost out of here, you stupid mother fucker!"

He said, "Why did you have to go and call the director? You stupid fucking cop! I was almost gone! I could have buried my dick in some more sweet, tight ass before they caught up with me if you hadn't called, you fucking idiot!"

I said, "By 'tight ass', you mean little babies. Is that what you mean, Mr. Robins?"

He glared at me and spit out, "Fuck Ya! Best ever! You can tell they want it! You should see their faces when I slide my dick in!"

I stepped back, amazed at the transformation; this was the real Mr. Robins. It was no wonder the Mountain had wanted to beat his ass.

I was shaking with rage and feeling sick.

Robins continued to spew venomous shit in my direction until the director arrived.

He walked in and looked at us, saying, "I see you have met the real Mr. Robins. Do you still need to see the documents?"

I said that I did and that he should show them to me.

He said that Mr. Robins had tried to escape many times and that he was one of their most difficult patients. He was sad about the abuse Mr. Robins had received and would make sure that it did not happen again.

I left the facility with my head spinning. I wrote up this surprising turn in the case and explained to the Sergeant what had happened.

He looked at me in disbelief as well. I cleared the case with dispatch and was told that I could now go eat; it was six hours later.

I had no appetite; I passed and went on to the next call, trying to put some distance between the sick, angry Mr. Robins and me.

Let Me Help You Out
Of That Shirt

THE POWERS THAT BE HAD made a decision, and I was on day shift; apparently, they needed to break up the "cliques" that had developed in the department. (Meaning the different squads were getting too close, too vocal against the administration's current botched attempts at management.) Sergeant Duke had been on mids (midnights) for years, and he was now on the other one of the two day shifts.

I was sent to straight days with the old timers, good dudes that had survived many administrations and many purges of personnel; solid old timers who had done their time on the street and had finally gravitated to day shift to finish out their tours, waiting for retirement.

They had forgotten more about the street than most of the new guys would ever learn. I was fortunate to have been "banished" to this group.

Like I have said before, the daylight hours are full of "Daywalkers," the people that spend their lives going to work, watching *Dancing With The Stars* at night, and driving minivans full of screaming kids to soccer and dance practice. They are not night people. They actually believe your job as a cop is to answer their questions, make their lives comfortable and safe. They drive me insane.

While I was sitting there one day in my patrol car, a guy rolled up and waved. Smiling—actually smiling—he got out of his car and walked towards me, not realizing, of course, that I was not a day cop.

I had already unholstered my gun, just in case the smile and wave were a ruse.

At night, no one walks up on a cop car—*never*, they know better.

At night, my windows are always down, and I am always listening. If I park, it is in a large parking lot or backed up to a fence in the corner of a vacant lot; no one is going to sneak up on me and put a bullet in my head without me having plenty of warning.

At night, that is the reality. In the daytime, all the lots are full, there is nowhere to park where you're safe, and the Daywalkers are out smiling and waving, unaware of the shit storm that surrounds them, walking up to ask you a question they feel must be asked—and naturally, you're there to provide the answer.

Anyway, Mr. Used Car Salesman approached, and my gun cleared leather. I waited, watching his hands and body language as he approached.

"Hi, officer, I'm wondering if you can answer a question?"

That's usually how it begins: smiling, wanting to shake my hand. He was baffled why I wouldn't return the gesture.

Watching his hands, I saw no calluses; there were manicured nails, gold jewelry proudly displayed, a nice watch, and a masculine gold bracelet worn on his wrist; a walking robbery victim begging to be robbed and beaten, if this were a night shift.

I relaxed a little bit, realizing that he was obviously soft, very soft—the kind of guy that folds up and shuts down if he's present during a robbery of his favorite jewelry store.

Later, though, he'll be in front of a camera, telling the reporters how he wanted to stop it, but couldn't, while the robbers raped the girl behind the counter. Every night cop knows the type.

The question he has to ask? It could be any of the following: "I need a battery for my cell phone—can you tell me where I can get one?"

"Do you know where the closest pay phone is?"

"Can you recommend a good restaurant?"

"Where is the nearest Laundromat?"

"Can you recommend a good mechanic?"

Seriously this is what Daywalkers think you're there for, a walking almanac of information at their disposal.

If he makes the *huge* mistake of telling me that he's the Chief's or Mayor's best friend?

Well, he's about to get directions all over the damn city, finally ending back at the nearest drug house or the worst neighborhood in the city that's nearby.

Never tell a street cop your BF is an administrator in the department, and then ask a question; just a bit of advice, take it or leave it.

Anyway, I was on days, and Mr. Soft Hands had been sent on his way. I was checking an apartment complex parking lot, looking for stolen cars that may have been dumped.

I saw a Chevy Tahoe approaching from the opposite direction, dark windows, two occupants. I could see immediately from the way they were sitting and acting that they are not civilians. Looking closer, I saw the hidden red and blues in the grill; law enforcement of some kind.

I pulled up and rolled down the window, then recognized the occupants: probation and parole officers hunting their lost sheep. We exchanged greetings. I knew the driver, who said to me, "What the hell are you doing off nights? I never thought I'd see you out in the sunlight." I muttered something about it's a long story and to drop it.

I asked them, "What's new? Who are you looking for in the area?" The driver handed me a picture of a 14-year-old girl who has been on the run for some time. They had been trying to find her for months. She was being "taken care of" by her boyfriend/pimp, and they were trying to get her locked up and cleaned up. They had heard from informants that she was staying in the apartment complex, but they didn't know exactly where.

They told me her history: abusive parents, drugs, sexual abuse by her brother and uncles.

They asked me to keep an eye out and if I saw her, tag her big time, then call them anytime and they'd come pick her up. They wanted to get her off the street before she ended up dead.

They also warned me that she's a runner.

I looked at the picture for several minutes, memorizing her face. The driver said I could keep the picture if I needed it. I said thanks, but no.

Once I have the face, it's locked in memory; I won't forget it. A few more looks at the picture, and I handed it back.

I asked them to tell me her name and DOB, this I had to write down. Faces are a lock, but names and dates of birth never; I can barely remember my own.

I got their cell numbers and told them I'd be on the look out. We then parted ways after exchanging a few insults about each other's departments.

Three weeks later, I was trolling the apartment complex. It had become a daily part of my routine. I had found three stolen vehicles in the lot and recovered them.

Day shift is clean up work, and this is the best I can hope for. Today I found no new stolen vehicles, and as I left the complex I saw a soft top jeep approaching.

I checked the driver to see if I knew him, and I didn't. Then I looked at the passenger: the lost and wayward 14-year-old girl was in the passenger seat. We made eye contact; it was definitely her.

I let them pass and enter the complex. I then pulled out of the complex and watched in my mirrors. They were watching me as well, making sure I pulled away.

Once they were no longer able to see me, I made a hard U-turn and accelerated; I was going to catch up to them when their guard was down.

Calling out the plate on the jeep as I turned, I told the dispatcher where I was and that I was out of the vehicle.

They had pulled into a parking place in the complex parking lot, so I pulled up fast and quiet. I blocked the jeep's escape and exited the patrol vehicle, locking the doors.

I then approached the passenger side of the jeep and started talking to the girl, telling the driver to keep his hands on the steering wheel.

He was about twenty-five, and probably a customer of the girl's. I explained to her that I knew who she was and that she was coming with me. She pretended to give up and unbuckled her seat belt.

As I opened the jeep's cloth passenger door, though, she was up and trying to go out the driver's door—over the top of the driver.

I reached in and grabbed her shirt, and it tore right off her; this is not what I had hoped for at all.

She was out of the vehicle and running, and I was thinking *Shit, I hate day shift.*

I started chasing her. I'm an armed officer in full uniform, chasing a shirtless, braless 14-year-old girl through an apartment complex common area.

The girl was wearing really short nylon shorts, pink and white tennis shoes, and her breasts were flopping in the wind.

To make matters worse, she started yelling for help and screaming, "Rape! Help me!"

Can things get any worse? Oh, hell yes they can!

Dudes started piling out of their apartments to see what the hell was going on, and women were yelling at me to leave the poor little girl alone.

Then I heard on the radio that dispatch was sending all available cars to the apartment complex on a report of a rape in progress.

There was a man in a security uniform chasing a naked girl through the complex. She said he'd raped her. That's the dispatch.

Now I was really pissed; no way this kid was getting away.

She ran all through the complex screaming rape, and when I didn't give up, she crossed the road and jumped into the nearby river.

By this time, I had a group of men chasing me as I chased her; guess they're gonna save her from the security guard rapist.

I jumped into the river as well, and I heard the patrol cars coming with sirens screaming and motors wound up. I'll never live this down! The old timers are ruthless in their pranks.

I waded across the river, which stops the crowd that was trying to get to me. The girl was already across the river and up on the bank.

She stopped to catch her breath, turned around, saw me, and started running again.

Fortunately, there was a guy on a mountain bike nearby. He rolled up as I crawled out of the river and said, "Do you want me to chase her down?"

I said, "Yes! Please!"

He asked what she had done, and I told him that she's on the run and being used as a prostitute by her boyfriend to make money and drugs; I was trying to get her out of that mess.

He was off and had her stopped in moments. I ran up and took her into custody.

I took off my uniform shirt and put it on her to cover her up. She turned and spit on me; so much for being a hero today.

I started to walk her back and explain to the responding units on the radio that I was the rapist security guard and that I had her in custody.

I had to walk her back across the river while the other units dispersed the crowd of "do-gooders" that had gathered to kick my rapist ass. (They wouldn't get wet and cross the river, however).

The duty Lieutenant walked up to me, pissed off and spewing venom. He said I had a lot of explaining to do and that I was in deep shit.

That was it! I lost it.

I replied, "Hey, do you know what the fuck you're talking about? Do you know what happened here? No, you don't have a fucking clue. You don't know shit! So why don't you man the fuck up and find out what happened before you decide I was in the wrong. Oh—and by the way, I'm fine, no injuries; thanks for asking." I walked off.

The Lieutenant had no comment—and the old timers?

Like I said, they'd forgotten more than this idiot would ever know. They all started laughing and jumped back into their cars, clearing the call.

I completed the paperwork, retrieved my shirt, and tried to dry off.

The Lieutenant made sure to get a statement from the half naked girl, asking over and over again if I'd tried to touch her in anyway that was sexual. To her credit, she said, "No."

The next day, the old timers bought me lunch, saying I'd earned it for putting the Lieutenant in his place. Day shift really sucked.

4 Cold Hearted Snake

I WAS WORKING CENTRAL CITY again, day shift, and finally had an in-progress call. It was just a domestic, but still, at least it was in progress.

The caller said that he was walking past a house in central city and could hear a woman and man fighting in the upstairs apartment. He said that he actually saw the man punch the woman in the face while he stood on the sidewalk outside the building. The caller then hung up, not wanting to be involved any further.

I arrived at the house, and all was quiet. My back up was a few minutes out, and I went in. The house was one of the older and larger homes that had been bought by one of the city's many slumlords. It had been renovated and was comprised now of several small apartments being let out at prices that drew the poor, elderly, and underachievers.

I entered the front door and listened. Nothing; not a sound.

Then a door opened upstairs, and an elderly woman looked out at me. She pointed at the apartment across the hall from her, nodded, then closed the door.

I advised my back up that the fight was in the apartment upstairs on the right, then quietly walked up the darkened stairs.

I waited outside the apartment, and I could hear people talking inside; several voices, no anger, just conversation between several voices.

I knocked on the door, and a voice said, "Come in." I opened the door and found I was in the living room of the apartment.

There were three couples sitting on the two couches in the living room, three men and three women.

One guy had his arm around a woman who was bleeding heavily from her nose. The blood was really flowing down her face and shirt as she sat there, her head down, and his arm was gently brushing her hair back out of her face.

The tension in the room was thick as I watched the others for their reaction. No one acted like anything was wrong with the situation; they just kept on talking as if this were normal. I asked the woman what had happened, and she didn't reply. I asked the man stroking her hair what had happened, and he said, "She fell down."

I asked her to get up and speak to me in the other room. She did this and told me that he was her husband and that he had regularly beaten her. She was afraid because he had threatened to kill her this afternoon when she told him she was leaving. She said that he told her he would never let her leave. Never.

I asked her if there were any weapons in the house, and she said that there were none but that all the people in the room were his family members, his cousins and their wives. She was afraid of what would happen if I tried to arrest him. I told her to let me worry about that and to stay in the back room while I talked to him.

I went back into the living room, and the guy was gone. The other couples were still there, talking as if nothing had happened.

I heard a noise in the bathroom and forced the door open; the guy was trying to force his fat ass out of a 1x1 window in the bathroom. No way that was gonna happen—he was way too big.

I stopped and watched while he tried and tried. I noticed he had a tattoo on the back of his neck that said "Cold Hearted Snake."

I finally said, "Hey, man, you aren't gonna ever get out that window. Just give up." He stopped and climbed out of the window and stepped out of the bathtub.

Then he tried to push past me; bad idea.

The fight was on right there in the hallway. I had him in a choke-hold pretty quick and told him to stop or I'd choke him out.

He stopped fighting but started yelling in Spanish to his cousins to come in and kill me.

Things were getting interesting. He wasn't gonna go without a fight.

One of his cousins appeared in the hallway, and they had a conversation in Spanish. The Cold Hearted Snake was telling his cousin that they could kill me and dump me in the alleyway behind the house. No one would know or tell on them. I was alone, and they could take me out.

I clamped down on the chokehold and told him to shut the fuck up.

I spoke directly to the cousin and told him I knew who he was and asked how his uncle Maldo was doing.

I told him that he'd better think it over before he decided to enter into this fight. He disappeared into the living room.

I figured that was a bad thing and that I had only a few seconds to get ready.

I had the Snake almost unconscious by then, and I dropped him to the floor, gagging and coughing. I cuffed him fast, then drew my gun and faced the direction the cousin had left.

He immediately reappeared, this time with a large knife in his hand.

I was calmer by now; this kind of combat was becoming the norm for me.

I talked to the cousin, calling him by his name.

"Remo, you need to think this over, ese. You know me, and you know I know you; no way you walk out of here alive if you take one more fucking step."

As I aimed at his head, he made eye contact with me and paused. He then dropped the knife on the floor and stepped back, hands up.

He said, "We cool?"

I replied, "Ya, we're cool, but this bitch is going to jail for beating his wife. You gotta accept that. You interfere, and I'll fuck you up."

I lowered my gun.

Remo began to talk to his cousin again in Spanish. He told him that he couldn't stop me from arresting him. He said that I knew him by name, and his uncle as well, and that he wasn't going to risk it.

He apologized, saying. "You're family, man, but I can't do this."

I holstered my handgun and picked the "Snake" up from the floor.

I started to walk him out, telling the cousin to get back in the living room. He did what I asked and backed into the room.

I made my way to the doorway of the apartment, watching every move made by the two remaining couples in the living room. They were agitated but not aggressive towards me.

The Snake was starting to get his wind back and started to resist me again.

I opened the door to the apartment, and the Snake yelled out in English that he had a thousand dollars for each of them if they stopped me from arresting him.

Then he said, "Kill this motherfucker now!"

I'd had enough. I looked at the two dudes on the couch, and they had an excited look on their faces; they were actually thinking that they could do this for money. Things were about to get real ugly as they quickly got up. Time to stop being so fucking polite.

I threw The Snake down the stairs, telling him to shut the fuck up. He screamed all the way down, tumbling and rolling head over heels, hands cuffed behind his back as he went down.

I turned and faced the approaching men and pulled my gun. I said, "Who's first? Who wants to die first, motherfuckers?"

They stopped. I was mad now. I said, "Bring it, bitches. A thousand dollars if you can take me. Who's first?"

They backed up. Remo said, "Hey, man. You just misunderstood, Pacman. We got no problem with you. Go ahead, ese, do your thing; arrest the bitch." They both wisely sat back down on the couch.

I heard the radios of my back up outside, then the front door of the house opened up.

The Snake was still lying on the floor at the base of the stairs, moaning. The back up officers drew their weapons, stepped over him, and rushed up the stairs.

The first officer there asked if I was OK. I replied that I was fine and that there was a woman inside who needed medical treatment.

They asked what happened to the guy at the bottom of the stairs. I told them he slipped and I couldn't catch him. I asked them to get statements while I transported the suspect to jail.

I went down the stairs and picked The Snake up from the floor. He was still fighting me, calling me a fucking punk and telling me he'd kill my ass when he got out of jail.

I told him I'd look forward to it as I put him in the car and took him to jail.

He wasn't done fighting, and I had to get help from the correctional officers to get him booked.

A couple days went by, and dispatch got a call from the old lady in the apartment next door to the Snake and his wife. She asked if I was on duty. They said I was, then she said that the Snake was back at the apartment; he was hitting the woman again, and she'd like it if I responded.

I was just around the corner when the call came in, and I asked dispatch to check and see if there was a protective order in effect for the couple. They checked, and there was an order; the Snake was violating it just by being there, and he was hitting her again.

I rolled up as he came running out of the house. He stopped, saw it was me, and took off behind the house.

I was out of the vehicle and chasing him. We jumped three fences and ended up in the alley that he wanted to dump my body in.

He took off down the alley, and as he was about midway to the street, another officer stepped into the alley and started walking up it.

The Snake was caught. He stopped, put his hands up, and said, "I give up! I give up!"

He put his hands on a nearby wall and said, "Just don't beat me up like last time."

The other officer overheard this and said, "What's he mean by that?"

I said that I didn't know; he must have me confused with someone else. I asked him to take Snake to jail while I went back and checked on the woman. He said that he would.

I went back to the apartment and found the woman inside. He had hit her again, and I obtained a statement from her and had CSI take photos of the new injuries.

As I was leaving, the old woman came out of her apartment.

She said, "Excuse me, officer."

I said, "Yes, ma'am?"

She said, "Aren't you the officer that was here last time?"

I said I was. She said, "And did you get him today?"

I said I had and that he was on his way to jail…again.

The old lady smiled and patted me on the arm. She said, "Young man, I like you! You have spunk! We need more police officers like you. Please come back and say hello some time."

I said, "Yes, ma'am."

I was stunned.

You forget working the street day in and day out that mixed in with the nightmare that is the street there are good people living in fear of shit bags like The Cold Hearted Snake.

She smiled at me and repeated, "Spunk!" making a tiny fist with her bony little hand and a little sparkle in her eyes.

I left and booked the Snake into jail. I never saw him again.

5 Can I Get You A Cup Of Coffee?

I WAS SITTING IN AN all-night restaurant one evening, eating and writing reports. I usually ate alone unless one of the very few cops I got along with was working, and then we might eat together.

Usually, you need the time alone to process the night, to try to make some sense out of the chaos and stupidity that seemed to be the norm. It almost never happened that you could get through an entire meal without the dispatcher asking you to clear for an in-progress felony or a bad accident; so, moments of peace and quiet are valued.

Still, if dispatch doesn't call you out, there's always at least one guy who sees you in the corner, backed against the wall, watching the door as you eat and write reports—hoping to never be caught unaware should all hell break loose right in front of you.

This guy just knows for sure that you're his newest long lost buddy, and he has a story to tell you or a really important question to ask.

Every cop knows exactly what I mean; the guy waves, smiles, and starts walking over to you, not noticing that your hand has quietly slipped to your gun and unsnapped the holster, clearing leather, just in case the smile is a ruse and this guy thinks he can get his face on CNN by killing you.

Usually, though, it's just a friendly question about some incident that happened or a guy that wants to know how he can get hired at the department; then he moves along.

This night I was writing reports, and I noticed an old guy walk in. I thought he looked familiar, but I couldn't place him.

I categorize people by threat in my memory, and this guy raised no alarms. He just seemed familiar.

Finally, after he saw me and headed over, I recognized him as a co-worker from another department. His name was Jake.

We used to work together before I went to the city and we'd stayed in touch. He had a wicked sense of humor, and we shared many funny stories about calls on the streets.

He sat down, and we started to talk and laugh. It was rare to laugh anymore; we'd both seen a lot and shared the camaraderie that you can only share with someone who has seen the same battles and knows what you feel and think without saying a word.

He kept shaking his head, and I knew that something was on his mind and waited to see what he would eventually spill; I didn't have to wait long.

He started by telling me that he'd been in a lot of trouble lately and thought for sure that he'd lose his job.

I thought this was an exaggeration, but he assured me that it wasn't.

He said that he had really "screwed the pooch" this time, staring off into space, chain smoking and drinking coffee.

I said, "Ya? So what did you do?"

He said, "Well, you knew I was promoted, didn't you?"

I said that I did know that and replied, "Why you ever wanted off the streets, I don't know. Now you're in the Administration and hating life, I bet?"

He replied that yes, he was now in admin as a Lieutenant and that he hated every day of it. He was on his last five years and took the job to increase his retirement income.

He went on and on about how he hated his boss and that he was constantly taking shit from the guy and keeping his mouth shut.

This was hard to imagine because he'd never been one to be silent about anything. I just listened and shook my head, thinking it wasn't worth it to promote in our field.

Then he lowered his voice and said, "Well, I'll tell you what I did— but you have to promise not to tell anyone!"

I said I would.

He paused for a few moments and continued. He said, "You know how I hated the son of a bitch before I was promoted. He was an asshole when you were at the department, and he's only gotten worse." Jake said, "I just had to do something to fight back."

I was quiet, thinking, *Wow, this could really be bad.*

Jake continued, "Well, you know how he used to come in every morning and get that same old coffee cup and get a cup of coffee, then start in on the people around him? Always complaining and talking down to everyone? No matter how bad the night had been, you could always do better in his eyes, and he felt it was his mission in life to point out every officer's mistake?"

I did know. The guy was a real prick, and no one liked him.

Jake said, "So one day after he was really riding me hard and calling me a fucking idiot, I'd had it! I made up my mind I was done taking his shit without doing something back."

Jake had my attention now. I could picture any number of scenarios going down, and he was capable of anything when he was pissed off.

I stopped eating, quit writing reports, and listened…Jake was really agitated. This was going to be good!

He said after the incident where the boss really chewed his ass, he came in early the next morning and picked up the Chief's coffee cup.

His beloved coffee cup hadn't been washed in years; he drank out of it every day and just rinsed it out, putting it back by the coffeemaker.

Jake said he took it to the bathroom and cleaned it out really good so that it looked like new.

I was puzzled. *WTF?*

I said, "You got back at him by kissing his ass and cleaning his coffee cup? You really have gone to the dark side and joined Admin!"

He laughed and said, "Noooo, I cleaned it out good and shiny, spotless as a matter of fact, and then took out my dick and rolled it around the rim of the cup—after taking a piss, of course! That way, every time the cup went to the Chief's mouth, I'd know his lips were touching where my dick had just been!!"

I burst out laughing. I hadn't laughed that hard in a long time. He laughed as well, and the entire restaurant stopped to look at us. We laughed hard and loud for a long time, both of our faces red, tears running down our faces.

I said, "So how long has this been going on?"

He said, "Three years!"

"Oh my god!" I laughed.

Finally, after I caught my breath, I said, "So what happened that you almost got fired?"

He said, "Well, I came in one morning and went to get his cup and headed for the bathroom to do my daily ritual, clean the cup, piss, and then swab the cup with my dick. I was almost done, and the door opened to the restroom. I'd always locked the door, but that day I forgot—and I looked up and there was the Chief!

"He looked at his cup in my hand, my dick still inside of it. He just stared at me, I looked back at him, and then we both looked at the cup.

"It was a really weird feeling knowing that we were both looking at my dick in the Chief's cup. No one said a word. He looked at me again then left the restroom."

I was barely able to breathe, I was laughing so hard!

Jake said, "I didn't know what to say, so I said nothing! We both stared at each other, and then at my dick in his cup. It was weird!"

After I caught my breath, and he stopped laughing as well, I asked what happened next.

Jake said, "Well, he didn't drink out of the cup that day—I can tell you that!" More laughter and tears.

Finally, he said the boss called him in and asked him how long he had been "cleaning his cup" that way. Jake said he lied and told him about a month.

Jake said that they came to an understanding. He, Jake, had to promise never to tell anyone this story; the boss didn't want anyone knowing that he'd been drinking out of a dick-swabbed cup.

Jake agreed, saying that he felt like he wasn't in a place to negotiate. (He had a wicked sense of humor). He said that as long as he agreed to keep his mouth shut, he could keep his job. He was given two days off without pay, and that was it!

I couldn't believe it! I said, "That was it? That's all you got?"

Jake said, "Yep, that was it."

Funny thing, though: now the boss treated him a lot different—and kept his coffee cup in his desk!

I laughed again. This was too funny not to share, but I'd promised never to tell.

The waitress came over and said to me, "I have never heard you laugh in all the years you've been coming in here, not once. I saw you smile once, but never laugh. What's so funny?"

I couldn't tell her—and if I did, she wouldn't think it was funny anyway. She just shook her head and walked off.

6 Feeling No Pain

ONE NIGHT, I WAS SENT to a domestic in an area where we never got those kinds of calls.

The area was an affluent one, where most of the residents competed with each other over who had the biggest boat or newest jet skis. They never called the cops about anything, so I knew it had to be pretty bad.

I arrived with a back up this time. We'd coordinated prior to arrival and arrived together, pretty much simultaneously. We walked up quietly, listening for any sound of a fight or disturbance; there was none.

After listening outside the front door for a moment I knocked, and a woman came to the door. She was beat to shit. She was bleeding from several wounds on her face and had a couple bald spots where her boyfriend had pulled her hair out. I asked her what had happened.

After several attempts to hide the truth, she told me that she and her boyfriend had been dropping acid and drinking. They'd gotten into an argument, and he'd just beat her up. Simple as that. She said when she got free from him, she grabbed the phone and called 911.

When he saw that she'd called, he took off.

She didn't want medical assistance and asked that we not call the paramedics for her. She said that she'd seek medical treatment on her own.

I asked her where her boyfriend might have gone. She said, "I don't know; he was so high, he could be anywhere."

Then we heard a noise in the basement, a loud crash.

I said, "What was that?" The woman said that she didn't know.

Both my back up and I went to the basement. After turning on all the lights, pretending that we had a dog, and announcing that we were going to send it in if the boyfriend didn't come out, several moments of silence passed—but nothing happened.

Finally, we decided we had to clear the basement and started down the stairs, guns drawn.

Before we went down, we asked the woman what her boyfriend's name was. She said his name was James Peebles, but that he thought of himself as a reincarnated James Dean. She said he'd only answer to 'James Dean Peebles'.

Great, we're going after an acid-dropping woman beater who thinks he's James Dean. Another typical night of weird shit.

We cleared the basement and found nothing. There was nothing out of place, no sight of the James Dean wannabe.

Then we heard a sneeze; soft and faint, but definitely a sneeze.

Shit! We looked at each other and thought, *what had we missed? Where could he be?* We looked around again and found nothing.

I called upstairs to the injured woman and asked her if there were any hidden areas in the basement. She came down the stairs and looked around and said, "Well, things have been moved. That large couple of boxes used to be over there, and now they're covering up the entrance to the crawl space."

I tried to move the boxes and found that they were very heavy; no one was in them, they were just heavy. It took a lot of effort by both me and the back up officer pushing them to move them.

Sure enough, there was a crawl space hidden behind the boxes. I saw that there was a light switch just inside in the dark and reached in and turned it on.

The crawl space lit up, we looked inside, and at the opposite corner all the way on the other end of the house was Mr. Peebles.

He was huddled up in a corner, facing away from us, pretending he wasn't there, I guess. We called to him several times, threatening to send a dog; he didn't budge.

Finally, we entered the crawl space, literally crawling on our hands and knees to get to Peebles. We were pissed off.

This was tactically dangerous, and besides that we were covered in dirt by the time we reached him. He didn't move until we were right on him—then the fight was on.

We outnumbered him two-to-one—and he was kicking our asses. He was high as hell and feeling no pain at all. Nothing worked; all the arrest control tactics we're taught as cops only work if the suspect is feeling pain—and Peebles felt nothing.

I had his arm behind his back in a wrist lock, and he didn't even notice. I cranked on the wrist until his hand laid flat against his forearm, palm laying flat against his own arm—and got no reaction at all.

I looked at my back up, and he looked at me, both of our eyes wide with surprise! We had to pull out all the stops and just brawl with Peebles until we had both hands cuffed. That only limited his ability to fight back.

We started to drag him from the crawl space, and he kicked and spit the entire way, slamming his own head into the floor joints above us.

About ten minutes later, we arrived at the opening of the crawl space, covered in dirt, sweat, and Peebles' blood and spit. We dragged him out of the crawl space—but he wasn't done yet.

He kept fighting as we pulled him out, growling like an animal and thrashing back and forth. His head went back and forth against the roughed-in 2x4 framed walls of the basement like a stick across a picket fence. He just didn't care. He felt nothing.

He continued to fight all the way to the patrol car.

Finally, we dropped him on the ground and shackled his feet. Grabbing a dog leash that everyone carried in their cars, we tied his feet to his wrists and dropped him in the back seat of the patrol vehicle. This was the only way to transport him at the time.

Years later, this tactic would kill several people, causing positional asphyxia; that night, however, it was the only way to control the acid-dropping Mr. Peebles. I booked him for the domestic assault and resisting arrest.

Two weeks later, I got a subpoena to go to court on Peebles. I arrived at court, expecting a brawl. I was beat to shit affecting the arrest of Peebles; he wasn't a big dude, but he felt no pain.

To make matters worse, I had to take my two-year-old daughter to court with me.

My wife at the time was convinced that I never did anything but write traffic tickets and help old ladies cross the street. She had an appointment to go to lunch with a friend and didn't feel that she should have to take our daughter with her.

She left me with the baby and said, "You'll be fine; you exaggerate so much! You big, tough man."

I walked in with my baby girl in my arms and asked the clerks to watch her. They said they couldn't.

I had to go into the courtroom with the crazed Mr. Peebles and my baby girl. I was on edge, ready to kill him if he even touched her.

I sat down, and the crazy fucker came right up and sat next to me; this was my worst nightmare.

I said nothing, and when they called the case, he stood up and said that he was present.

The prosecutor called me up, and Peebles turned to me. He said, "You're the one that arrested me?"

I said yes.

He looked at me for a moment, and I was sure we were gonna fight right there, but then his face changed.

He said, "I'm very sorry about that night. It must have been one hell of a fight, huh?"

I said, "Yes, it was."

He said that he didn't remember a thing, but the next day when he woke up, he could barely move.

He said to me, "What happened to my wrist? Jesus, it still hurts!"

I smiled and said again that it was a hard fight, all the while keeping my daughter behind me. He said again that he was sorry and that he just wanted to apologize.

He pled guilty to the charges, and I got the hell out of there, keeping myself between him and my baby girl.

When I finally did arrive home, I was still mad.

I began to argue with my wife about leaving me with our daughter.

She said, "Oh, you're just such a tough guy in your head, I know, but we both know your job isn't that dangerous!"

7 Sesame Street

THE DRUG DEALERS IN THE city had a street they referred to as "Sesame Street."

It was a dead end street off a main drag that was known for its drugs, prostitutes, and crime. It was well known that everyone was high as hell, and if anything happened you were on your own. None of the people who frequented the street would help anyone else. It didn't matter what it was that happened; you'd better be able to handle your own business.

Sesame Street was a dead end in more ways than one for a lot of people. It earned the nickname 'Sesame Street' from the theme song from the kids show, referring to the magical place where everyone was nice and the air was clean. Our Sesame Street was the exact opposite.

One evening while working night shift, we got an anonymous call of a fight that had broken out on Sesame Street. If we did get a call about the street, it was always just like this: anonymous, and almost always very bad.

Two cars rolled to the street to see what was up. They arrived and went to the address reported by the caller. One guy was focused on the house, the other was his back up. We were running short on manpower, as usual.

If the citizens knew how thinly spread we really were at that time, they would have freaked out.

Late at night, most every night, we were cut back to six guys for the entire city; amazing, but true. We could barely keep up with the in-progress felony calls, much less do anything preventive.

Anyway, the two cars arrived and went to the house and found Bubba Johnson and his elderly father in a fight.

Bubba had beaten up his dad pretty bad. Dad was no slouch, though. He'd put up a good fight, and the two of them had destroyed the house, breaking furniture, glass tabletops, and windows.

Our biggest problem was that they'd broken the natural gas-fueled wall heater that heated the house.

The two officers removed the elderly father to awaiting paramedics, then went back to go get Bubba.

He was barricaded in a bathroom and refused to come out. They finally coaxed him out.

He was high (as usual), and when they tried to arrest him, he fought back. He beat the hell out of the two officers, throwing them around the house, ripping the badge off one of them and stabbing him with the pin on the back of the badge.

They managed to call for more units, and I was available and went in immediately.

When I arrived, the fight was still in full swing. Bubba was a good-sized dude and was feeling no pain. He wasn't going to go without a battle. He kept trying to get to a gas oven that was in the house and light it; he wanted to kill us all.

To make matters worse, he had full-blown AIDS. He'd contracted it sharing a needle and knew his time was limited. He just didn't care about living or dying.

I jumped in, and being fresh and not fatigued from the battle, I was able to get him at least pinned against a wall with both arms behind his back.

The other two officers were injured, and the gas was still pouring out into the house; any spark at all, and we were all dead.

I told them to get out and get treatment.

I had Bubba off the ground with his arms behind his back and his toes barely touching the ground, pinned against the wall. The shift Sergeant arrived and began to help me arrest Bubba.

As soon as I let his feet touch the floor, the fight was back on; this time, however, I was fresh, and the Sergeant was an old timer, Kenny Duke. He had been in the department a long time, and he knew how to handle himself. He was older, but tough and not afraid to mix it up with anyone.

I wrestled Bubba to the ground and was able to get one hand cuffed, but not the other. The Duke came at him from the other side, trying to get his arm to where we could cuff him; Bubba wouldn't give in.

Duke looked at me smiled and said, "This is why they call it Sesame Street! Are you having fun yet?"

That's how he was: calm as hell in the middle of a battle and joking, even though at any minute the house could blow up from the gas leak and kill us all.

Duke said, "Time to quit fucking around with this guy."

We were on the floor on our knees, leaning over Bubba. He drove his right knee deep into Bubba's ribs.

Bubba cried out, but he wouldn't give us his hand. Duke kneed him again, harder this time. I heard a rib snap, but still Bubba wouldn't give in.

Duke looked at me, with surprise on both of our faces; Bubba was really high and feeling nothing.

Duke pulled his leg as far back as it would go and drove it deep into Bubba's ribs. I heard many snaps and pops that time, and Bubba finally had a change of heart and gave in.

We cuffed him and got the hell out of the house.

Once we were clear, we advised Fire that the scene was secure, and they came in and turned off the gas.

The other two cops had received several minor injuries from their fight with Bubba. One had to get the stab wound, that he received from being stabbed with his badge, treated.

Bubba's father had to be admitted to the hospital for his injuries as well. Bubba was transported to the hospital for the broken ribs and was later booked into jail for the incident.

Any call we went to on "Sesame Street" was always an interesting time.

8 Warned But Ignored

ONE DAY, I GOT A call from a guy who wanted to talk to an officer. It wasn't a priority call. He called dispatch and asked them to send a cop to his house because he had a question to ask.

I went to his house at the very end of a dead end street. He was sitting on his porch, watching the neighborhood kids playing in the street. As I walked up, he never took his eyes off the kids; he just stared at them and spoke to me.

I asked him what he needed to talk to a cop about. He took off his glasses, and I saw that he had tears slowly rolling down his cheeks from both eyes. He said, "Officer, I need your help......I need your help right now before something bad happens."

I was expecting the usual: he had access to a secret plot by aliens to kill the president, or maybe signals from space were telling him of an impending alien invasion. This was how those kinds of calls usually started out.

I told him, "Sure, I'll help you in any way I can, sir," already noticing he had no weapons and that his hands were in plain sight. I had him stand up and checked all around him; no weapons.

I let him sit back down and prepared to listen to his story about the aliens; I was wrong, though—this was no story about aliens.

The guy told me his name was Rory Adams. He was on disability and living in a small trashed apartment. He says that until recently he had been fine, nothing had been wrong, and then one day he started to have "uncomfortable feelings." He was quiet.

I said, "Uncomfortable feelings? About what?" He didn't answer me for some time. He just sat, breathing in large gasps and sobbing.

He said, "Please believe me. I'm getting really strong feelings that I'm going to harm someone."

I was paying attention. Serious attention. We rarely had a warning from someone before they went off the deep end and harmed others. This guy was asking for help, and he was seriously upset.

I told him that I would do whatever I could to help him. I asked him if he had any urges to hurt someone specific. He said that he really wanted to take one of the kids he had been watching in the street and "harm them."

I now realized why he was "target locked" on the kids playing in the street as I walked up, as well as why he was crying; he didn't want to harm them, but he was having some kind of psychological issue that made him want to hurt them. He was asking for help, afraid of what he might do.

This was a first for me. Usually, cops were in reactive mode, always going to a call after something had happened; here was chance to stop it before it happened, and I planned on making the most of it.

I told him that I would take him to the hospital and have him involuntarily committed. The laws at the time allowed a cop to commit a person who was suicidal to a hospital psych ward. I explained this to him, telling him that the only way I could get him any help was that I had to hear him say he was suicidal, using those words.

He reached out his hand to me, asking me to take his hand. (This was a major tactical *do not* do.) I allowed him to hold my hand, however, and while he cried, he said, "Thank you," and "Yes, I am suicidal."

We both knew that he was not suicidal, but that was the only way I could get him off the streets. He had broken no laws, and there was no facility for people who *might* break the law. The psych ward was all I had as a resource. I handcuffed him and took him to the hospital.

Driving past the children playing on his street, he breathed a sigh of relief. He said over and over, "Thank you, thank you."

We arrived at the hospital, and I explained in great detail the nature of his problem to the psych workers, adding that he had told me that he was suicidal.

It was not a lie; he had told me that after I had coached him. They agreed to accept him. They really had no choice; by law, they had to keep him twenty-four hours.

I left the hospital and felt pretty good about myself. I wrote up the report in more detail than I normally would, just in case something did ever happen, making sure I added in his request and his telling me that he wanted to harm the neighborhood kids.

I went on to the next call and forgot about Rory.

About a month later, I got a call at home. Detectives were working the case of a missing juvenile female. She had been abducted from the same street Rory Adams lived on. She had last been seen with Adams, and when the detectives pulled Adams up on the computer, they found my case report. They asked me if I felt he was a real threat.

I replied that he was and that I had believed him enough to commit him to the psych ward. I told them that I had explained everything to the psych worker that night and added his information to the report as well.

They said that they had read the report, contacted the hospital, and that they said Adams was no threat; they felt he just wanted attention. I strongly disagreed.

I was pissed off. In spite of all I had done, he still did not get treatment; instead, he was freed without receiving meds or therapy, given a stamp of approval by the psych ward and let loose. Now he had abducted a little girl, and they were gone. I was sick. This shit really sucked.

I went to work that night and spent the night looking for Adams in-between calls.

This was before Amber Alerts, and the Internet was still relatively new. Cops didn't use it yet; however, we got on the phone to the late night radio DJs and asked that they announce his car description, license plate, and his name on their radio stations. It would get us fired if we were caught, but honestly no one cared. We all felt we had to do everything possible to find this little girl.

Adams was found later the next day. He had raped the little girl repeatedly. She was found in his car, tied up in the back seat, about 150 miles away on a rural road.

He went a month later to court and told them he had asked for help repeatedly, recalling our conversation and the report I wrote. He had warned us, but no one listened. I was frustrated beyond belief.

This is what the street is all about for cops: trying to make a difference—and rarely do we really succeed.

9 Take Time To Unplug

IF YOU HAVEN'T FIGURED IT out by now, I have never followed the rules. I thought I'd throw that out there.

One night I went to work, and the day started out like any other day: briefing on the latest stolen cars, people we were looking for, rapists and robbers, then we all sat down and discussed what had happened the night before. The Sergeant assigned was Leeds. (Again I was working for this dickweed.)

Afterward, we went out to hit the streets. First call out of briefing was a suicidal woman at the local hospital Emergency Room. She was being admitted to the psych ward and wouldn't go without a fight. The hospital security guards were having a hard time with her and needed help.

I arrived with the plan of stuffing her into a straight jacket and being out on the street in five minutes or less.

We had a saying on the street: "If you're talking about suicide, you're not serious."

The only people serious about suicide were those that were dead when we arrived; the rest we felt were just attention whores and pussies who couldn't cope in life. This call forever changed that in my mind.

I arrived to find a quiet woman about forty years old sitting in a chair. She refused to get up to go to the psych ward. She wasn't violent or abusive; she just wouldn't go.

The security guard was uncomfortable with her because she was pretty and she intimidated him. He didn't want to lay hands on her for fear of a sexual harassment suit.

The nurses didn't know what to do, so they called and expected me to make her go. I was briefed by them that she had been committed by her family because she was truly suicidal. We called it a "Blue Slip" back then: family members could commit her on a blue slip.

I started with the usual line that she could get up willingly or I would make her get up. The five minutes was ticking past, and I wanted to be out on the street.

She calmly looked up at me and said, "If you want to make me go, I have no doubt you can. It won't change a thing; when I leave here, I will kill myself—and there is nothing you or anyone else can do."

She wasn't afraid or emotional; she was very matter-of-fact, almost business-like. I looked at her long and hard. This was no cry for help. She wasn't upset; she was resigned, determined, and her mind was made up.

Rory Adams was still fresh in my mind. I had no confidence that the psych ward would be able to help her any more than they helped him.

Several minutes passed with us staring at each other, neither saying a word. Our eyes were locked in a staring match I have never forgotten.

Finally, I asked her if she'd walk with me and talk away from the hospital. I told her I'd give her my word that I wouldn't force her to go to the psych ward; I just wanted her to walk with me.

She stared at me another thirty seconds or so then quietly said, "OK."

We walked out the Emergency Room door, went to a nearby bench, and sat.

I pulled the radio I carried off my belt and told dispatch I'd be busy at the hospital and unavailable, then I turned off the radio completely.

I told her, "You have my full attention. I'll be in deep shit for this with my bosses, but I want to understand what it is that has you at this point."

She told me her story: her husband had killed himself about three months earlier, leaving her with three teenage kids. She was devastated by his death, and she felt betrayed by him. In the same breath, she felt terrible loss and wanted to be with him. She loved him dearly and felt that maybe if she killed herself they'd be together "somewhere else."

She said that her children didn't need her now; all they did was fight with her, and no one cared how she felt.

Finally, one day she decided that she'd just kill herself. Her parents and friends saw the change in her and elected to have her committed to the psych ward, where the experts would help her.

We talked for six hours. During that time the nurses came out to see if I needed anything. I asked them to leave us alone. After the first two hours had passed, they finally got the message and left us alone.

I told her that I agreed with her that no one could stop her from killing herself. If she wanted to do it, nothing would stop her. I told her about our rule on the street about suicidal people and that I had planned to stuff her in a straight jacket and move on. I changed my mind, though, when I saw her attitude was like a cancer patient that has no hope for remission. She had resolved herself to dying, and I couldn't let that just happen without trying to talk to her.

I told her about my life and the trials I'd experienced. Several times, I'd thought about blowing my brains out as well. The horrors of the street, several broken marriages, and now the estrangement I had with my daughter had taken its toll. I really didn't give a fuck about much.

I told her how I'd been hopping hot calls on the job, going from shooting to stabbing, hoping to get into some shit that would let me die on the job, hopefully in a battle.

I didn't want to die a frail old man, shitting myself in a hospital bed, surrounded by my children—who wouldn't want to be there to begin with. I wanted to go out on my own terms just like she did, by my own choice.

She was shocked by this. She took the offensive and told me I had no right to make that choice; I was a cop, and I was supposed to protect people.

I laughed hard at that.

I told her I used to feel the same way 'til a tiny baby girl was shot a couple feet from me in a drive-by shooting. I felt that no way anyone would try some shit like that knowing I was there—but they had. I hadn't protected anyone.

I told her about Rory Adams and how I tried to keep him from harming the kids on his street—but I couldn't; he still raped a little girl.

I told her about going into a blood-splattered apartment where a child had been beaten and kicked to death by a babysitter, seeing pieces of the infant scattered around the apartment—and not being able to do a thing to make that right either.

I told her about sitting in a parking lot at Christmas time, talking to a friend while a woman was beaten to death with a hammer by her husband a block away. I did nothing to stop that, so how could she think I protected anyone from anything?

She had no answer. She said, "What keeps you going, then?"

I told her, "For me, it's the battle, the possibility that tomorrow I might make a difference. I might stop a murder or a rape, I might make that day worth living."

That was the only thing that I looked forward to, the only thing that separated her from me.

We sat there sharing stories about our kids, and I told her about several of the more difficult emotional cases I had worked and how they'd impacted me.

We laughed about Sergeant Gus calling the chief by accident, and she cried about the girl who was raped by her boyfriend and cut up with a knife.

Finally, we stopped talking, both of us staring straight ahead.

I said, "I'm going to have to commit you to the psych ward just from what you've told me. I know they won't do a damn thing to stop you, but I'm required to do it by law. I just want you to know that up front. I appreciate that you've talked to me and told me about your life.

If you do decide to kill yourself, I'll respect that. It's your life. You can do as you wish."

As we walked back in, she thanked me for talking to her for so long.

She said, "I hope that you don't get into too much trouble."

I said that I didn't care; the police department had forgotten long ago what this job is about. We're supposed to be here for people—that's everyone, not just the wealthy and sane, but the crazy and poor as well.

I suggested that she take it day by day…just make it through the next moment. That was what I'd learned to do on the street: survive the moment and then the next, 'til the shift is over and you've earned the right to go home to your kids.

She looked at me and said she'd think about it. I asked her to send me a card in a year or two if she made it through this hard time and let me know that she didn't kill herself and to tell me how it had turned out.

She gave me a funny look and walked away with the psych workers.

I went back to work. Sergeant Leeds was furious and called me a "sand bagging lazy fucker" for milking the call so long. He asked what the call was about, and I told him.

He rolled his eyes and said, "Jesus, you're not a fucking social worker!"

I told him, "Write me up, then!"

I'd given up on pleasing his ass long ago. I just didn't give a shit what he thought about anything.

About two years later, I came to work and an envelope was in my box. It had no return address and had a thank you card and a picture inside. It was from the suicidal woman at the hospital.

She said she was still taking it day by day. She enclosed a picture of her grandson, an infant maybe six weeks old. She said, "Without you, I never would have seen him. Thanks again."

Once in a very rare while, you felt like what you did actually mattered.

10 Fishing At The Ole Fishing Hole

IT WAS ABOUT 7 P.M. ONE summer night when I got this call.

I was dispatched to contact the parents of a 10-year-old boy. They were homeless and living in one of the many low rent motels in the more rundown parts of the city.

The hotel had been built on the banks of a river, and in its day it was fairly nice. Its trademark was a huge water wheel, similar to the wheels that supplied power to saw mills and granaries using water power to turn the huge wheel instead of electricity. The wheel had long since quit turning and was now just for show.

I arrived at the motel and contacted the manager. I asked him about the occupants of the room I was being sent to see, trying to find out if he knew anything about them.

Being sent to similar motels had made me cautious, and I never went directly to the room anymore. I always checked with the manager first to see if the room was even occupied; I took nothing for granted.

The manager said the occupants were a family of four. They had been in the motel for about two months, and he never had any problems with them. He said that they had been ideal tenants.

I went to the room and contacted the parents. The father asked if we could talk outside the motel room, so we stayed outside.

He said that they were, in fact, nearly homeless. He had lost his job, and then their house; they had been forced to move into the motel while he looked for work. He said that his son had been frequenting the river bottoms and hanging out, fishing with some friends he had made with the "Bo's" in the area for the past 4 weeks. He said something had happened yesterday and that his son came home crying after spending the entire day fishing with his friends, the "Bo's."

I said, "By 'Bo's', you mean hobos? Transients?" He said yes.

I already knew this was not going to be good. People have been fed a line of shit by the media that there is no difference between hobos or transients and homeless people. There is a huge difference.

Transients are not homeless due to circumstances beyond their control; they choose to be that way. Most are severely mentally ill, dangerous, and a lot of them are on the run for crimes they've committed. Hiding in the homeless world is easy for criminals.

Anyway, the father asked that I interview his son and find out what had happened. He said that he was worried "something bad had happened" and that his son had refused to talk to him.

I spoke to the boy and asked him if he would talk to me in my car. His demeanor was very disturbing. He looked emotionally shattered, broken, and barely keeping himself together.

I could tell that I wasn't going to do the kid any good by forcing him to tell me what had happened. He was broken by whatever had happened to him, so I started out by talking to him about fishing, asking him what type of fishing he did.

"Have you ever fly fished? Are you a bait fisherman?" He brightened up and started to talk.

I then let him know that I was familiar with the river bottoms and told him about a fight I had with a huge transient about ten years earlier who had wanted to kill me.

I told him that I had always thought hobos were cool until that moment; I had been raised in an era where people thought of hobos as harmless simple-minded folks who wore patched clothes and were more like clowns than criminals. I found out differently when I started to work as a cop.

He was quiet listening to this.

I recalled how a clown had been at a birthday party when I was a kid. The clown was dressed as a hobo. So that was what I expected when I first met them: harmless happy guys who would do tricks. (Of course, this wasn't what I really believed, but it made sense in a kid's world.)

He nodded and said, "Exactly!"

He started to tell me that he'd been befriended by a group of five or six men who lived in the river bottoms. They'd talked to him as a friend and treated him with a fatherly kind of attention.

He had fished with them and learned how to clean a fish after he caught it, learned to build camp fires, and he listened to their stories about living the life on the road.

I agreed that that sounded great. I asked how long he'd been fishing with them.

He said that he met them about three weeks ago and that they'd introduced themselves with their road names. (Cowboy, Boots, Whistler, Sticks, and Cookie.)

He recalled shaking each man's hand and feeling like the group accepted him. He said he'd spent every spare moment in the river bottoms and rail yards, hanging out with his new friends.

When I could tell that we'd established some trust, I started to pry into what had happened the day before.

I asked him, "So what happened yesterday? What went wrong?"

His demeanor immediately changed from happy 10-year-old boy to broken, damaged kid.

He was quiet for about five minutes, and I said nothing at all and let him work up the courage to tell me what had happened.

Finally, he started to talk.

He said that he went fishing in the morning and ran into his friends at about 10 or 11a.m. They were fishing as well and bathing in the river.

He said he could tell something was different about them, but he didn't know what.

He finally asked, and they told him that they were going to leave that day and hit the road. They said it was time to move on.

He said he was sad and asked them not to leave, telling them that they were about the only friends he had.

They said that they had the "itch"; they'd been in one place too long, and it was time to go.

He said all five of the men were swimming in the water, and they invited him to join them. He stripped down and jumped in the water with them then a couple of them got out and started to break camp.

They then went into the woods nearby and brought back a large log to sit on. Finally, they all were out of the water, getting dressed. The two guys that had gotten out of the water first grabbed him.

He thought that they were playing with him; they weren't.

The three men took turns raping him anally while the two men held him bent over the log. He said they held a knife to his throat and told him that if he cried out for help, they'd cut his throat and dump him in the river.

They did cut him slightly on the arm, just to emphasize the point.

After they took turns raping him, they then made him sit on the ground on his knees and give each of them a blowjob while someone held a knife to his throat.

Listening to him sob and cry, I was sickened by what he'd been through. He said that when they were finished with him, they made him get in the river and stay there to clean off the blood, shit, and semen.

They then took his clothes and hid them, packed up, and hopped on a train.

They told him to wait 'til the train was out of sight before he got out of the river or they'd come back and kill him.

He did what they said. Then he got out of the river and searched for his clothes. Eventually, he made his way home, broken and betrayed.

His parents could tell something had happened; usually he was happy and had stories to tell them about the hobos and their exciting life, but he came home that day quiet and trembling from the day's events.

He said that he felt dirty, and he couldn't understand why they'd done that to him.

I spent the next hour helping him process the rapes, making him realize he wasn't to blame.

I told him I would have to tell his dad and mom and asked if that was OK with him. He eventually said that it was OK, but he knew they'd think it was his fault.

When I explained to his parents what had happened, the father threw up and the mom just sobbed.

I told them I wanted to have their son submit to a rape kit, but they refused. They didn't want a report made. They didn't want this to be recorded anywhere.

I told them I wouldn't be able to convict the men if they didn't cooperate. They didn't care. They just wanted to ignore the event, and they asked me to leave—now!

I left and went to the rail yards. I found the camp and the log that the boy had been raped on. There was nothing around, no evidence, no cans, foot prints—nothing.

I went back to the motel the next day to see if I could get the family to change their minds about cooperating with an investigation, but according to the manager, they'd checked out in the middle of the night. He said they couldn't pack fast enough and that they were very rough with the boy, telling him he should have known better.

The manager asked, "What did that mean? What should the boy have known better about?"

I said nothing; I just shook my head and got into my car.

This wasn't an event that they could pretend never happened. The kid had done nothing wrong.

I drove around for a while in a smoldering rage, wishing I could find the transients, but at the same time knowing I could never make this right.

11 Nobody Rides For Free

BECAUSE OF MY AREA, I was in the Emergency Room a lot.

There was a lot of violent crime in the area, and like I've mentioned before, a lot of people with various mental illnesses.

Cops and ER nurses are like two prize fighters sizing each other up: each is able to land fatal blows, knowing the other is a shadowy reflection of what could have been. Both are adrenaline junkies, both think on their feet, and both play by their own rules.

I became friends with several of the ER nurses, and immediately the pranks started. We started out with small stuff, but eventually we were into some serious "destroy-your-life" stuff; no holds barred.

For example: one night, I brought a really combative suspect to be treated at the hospital before he was booked into jail.

The jail wouldn't accept injured prisoners, and this guy had put his fist through a window and nearly severed his arm. He was drunk, abusive, and bleeding like hell. I'd wrestled him down and contained him, then stuffed him into an ambulance.

They took him to the ER, and I followed them in case he got wild in the back of the ambulance.

While we were waiting, one of the nurses that I was in a constant battle with walked past and said, "That guy is a mess, was he a hard one to get here?" I said he was.

I was still a little bit shook up over the battle. He was feeling no pain and bled all over me.

She said, "Hey, I'm going to get a drink. Do you want me to bring you one?"

I said, "Sure, please."

I pretended not to be suspicious, but by now I trusted no one; anyone who was nice to me while I was in uniform was suspect.

She came back a few minutes later with an opened can of Coke. I said thanks and left it on the tabletop while I wrote reports. She came back two times in five minutes to see how I was.

If I were on "Lost in Space", Robot would have been yelling: "Danger, Will Robinson! Danger! There is a crazy woman nearby!" I heard the robot loud and clear.

I kept writing, and after she left I poured about half of it out in a nearby sink and moved the can.

She came back, I looked up, and she smiled and said, "Doing OK?"

I said, "Yes, thanks for the drink."

She smiled and said, "Anytime." She then left.

About twenty minutes later, another nurse walked past. She was a good friend. We'd sparred briefly and both realized that this would be a no holds barred death match.

Finally, she asked me to meet her at the ER one night and called a truce.

She said, "I'm calling a truce. I realized after your last prank that we're gonna end up killing each other; neither of us plays by the rules, and neither of us will back down. I'm asking you to stop. Truce?"

I said, "Sure, truce—but you cross me, and it's back on."

She never did, and we became good friends with mutual respect for each other's abilities as pranksters.

Her name was Tori. I called her Scary Tori 'cuz like me, she had an evil sense of humor.

Anyway Scary Tori said to me, "Did you drink that can of Coke?"

I said, "Absolutely not. Do I look stupid?"

She smiled and said, "I knew you wouldn't."

She told me that the other nurse had laced the drink with a diuretic and that had I drank it, I would have been peeing for hours.

I said, "Ya, well she was way too nice. I knew something was up."

Unlike my peers, I didn't think I deserved special treatment for being a cop and actually expected to be treated poorly. So when someone was nice (especially a beautiful nurse), the Robot came out waving his arms, and shields were up.

I got my payback, and the caring, concerned nurse also called a truce (wisely), apologizing and promising never to spike a drink again.

A few weeks later, the ER had a new clerk. I came in a few times, and she had heard about the pranks.

She was really cocky and thought of herself as a princess. She was out to prove that she could handle whatever I dished out.

She said one night, "I heard you're scary! You don't look so scary!"

The nurses around her started to scatter. I ignored her.

She said, "Yep, just what I thought—all talk!"

She then waddled away. I shook my head.

I went up to the cafeteria where the hospital workers ate and bought lunch, eating while I finished my report. When I returned to my car, it was buried in snow. I walked back in the ER, and Tori came to me and said, "I told her this was a really bad idea, but she wouldn't listen."

I said, "Where did she get the shovels to move the snow?"

Tori smiled a huge smile and said, "Well, I can't lie; I told her where they were. I think I'm going to like seeing the princess put in her place—but I did tell her not to do it."

I cleaned off my car and drove away.

No way this plump dairy princess would be able to hang, so I let it go. I parked in another lot the next time I went up to the hospital to eat. This worked for a short period, until one night I returned to my car—and it was covered in toilet paper. Seriously, this was her idea of a prank? Toilet paper? Maybe in 6th grade!

I had a reserve riding with me that night. (Jeff Mckell again.) I told him he should probably go home.

He said, "No, man—I heard about your pranks! I wanna see what you'll do."

I said, "Are you sure?" He said he was.

I said, "OK, no matter what—no statements; you didn't see anything. Understood?"

He said, "Sure!"

I went back to the ER and looked at the Princess' nametag. She smiled at me, and her double chin jiggled as she tried not to laugh. She had a little cat-shaped pin on her lapel, and I noticed the eraser on her pencil was also a cat.

The woman liked cats. Hmmmm. Tori saw the look in my eyes and raised her eyebrows. She held up her hands, said, "I'm out of this!" and walked away.

I went to my car and told Jeff, "Last chance!" He just laughed and said, "I'm all in."

Getting out of the patrol car, I called up dispatch and asked for the on-call animal control officer's phone number. I called her at home, waking her up.

Keep in mind, it's 3 a.m.. Did I care? No, this is all-out war now.

I asked the sleepy worker where they kept the dead cats after they put them to sleep. She said in a barrel, then when the barrel was full they'd burn them. She said the barrel was in the back of the complex and that the entire animal control complex was fenced and locked. No one was there.

I said, "OK, thanks."

She asked why I wanted to know, and I said, "Never mind. It's a dumb question. Good night!" The sleepy animal control worker went back to sleep.

I pulled two black plastic garbage bags out of the trunk of the patrol car and drove to the animal shelter. I got out, and Jeff saw the bags. His first thought was that I was going to burglarize the animal control shelter. He was really upset.

He had a pending job offer at a nearby police department, and now he thought he was witnessing a burglary-in-progress by another cop. He pleaded with me to stop, but I ignored him and jumped the 10-foot-high fence.

I went to the back of the complex and dumped out the barrels, picking out six of the most disgusting of the dead cats. I double-bagged them and came back to the car.

Jeff saw that the bag was full and put his head in his hands. I put the cats in the trunk and got in the car. Jeff was nearly in tears.

He said, "Zach, please! I don't wanna go to jail; just take the money back. I won't say a thing!"

I realized he was serious! I laughed. This was too sweet! Two pranks for the price of one.

I started the car and turned on the radio, and "Ratt" came blaring over the radio, singing "Nobody rides for free!" This was karma! I started singing the song and driving like crazy.

Meanwhile Jeff is watching his future go down the toilet; his degree will mean nothing now. In his mind, his dream of being a cop one day is over.

I hauled ass back to the hospital and found the dairy princess' car. It wasn't hard to find; when I was on the phone with dispatch, I had them run her name and got the plate for her car, a purple Dodge Neon. The personalized plate? It said PURR.

In five minutes, I had the car opened, the cats strategically placed near the floor heater vents (but out of sight), and the car locked back up.

I returned to the car, and Jeff was elated! He said, "It was just cats? No money, just dead cats?"

I said, "What the hell, man? You think I'm gonna burglarize the animal shelter?"

He laughed a giddy, nervous laugh, then said, "Zach, with you I never know what's gonna happen." Then he mumbled, "I get to keep my job; it was just dead cats." He was seriously traumatized.

The princess warmed her car up because she didn't like to be cold. She did this every night before she went home; so, when she came back to her car, the dead cats were thawed and oozing all over the car's carpet. She lost her mind when she found the first one, and six cats later she was crazy with rage.

Tori told me that she took her aside and said, "I told you don't mess with him. This is stage one; you don't wanna play this game. Stop now while you can."

She asked Tori to tell me she was stopping, that the game was over, no more pranks—which she did.

I went into the ER a few days later with another wacked out Tweeker to be treated, and while I was writing my report the princess sat down near me.

I made a soft "Meeoow" sound that only she could hear. She threw her papers at me and left the room.

The Princess eventually had to sell her car; she never could get the smell out of the carpet.

12 Wanna Go For A Ride?

FOR MOST COPS, A RIDE-ALONG is a pain in the ass.

You get some college or high school kid that has taken a course or two and is now an expert in the law enforcement.

Even worse, if your luck is really bad, you get the Criminal Justice major—the expert in all things law enforcement—commenting on your every traffic stop, every interview, evaluating your probable cause, and critiquing your abilities as a cop.

During my career, I had a few ride-alongs. Most were short-lived and moved on to friendlier, more patient officers. You get in my car and change the radio station, adjust the heater or air conditioner, then sit back and begin to critique my work—and you will find your ass on the side of the road in a bad part of town. If you're lucky, I *might* at least take you back to your car before telling you in no uncertain terms to get the hell out and don't bother coming back.

In my mind, the whole damn concept of a ride-along is flawed. It's the police department's idea of public relations. They require the ride-along to sign a waiver, releasing the department from liability should anything happen to them, and then they hop in the car. Smiling, shiny faces hoping to see some real action, have some "cop" experience to brag about to their classmates or friends.

Reality is, every night the cop goes out, he is armed, trained, and wearing body armor.

Every night, he is on guard the entire night, watching hands, eye contact, looking for weapons on every person he meets; listening not only to what every person he comes into contact with says, but how it is said, acutely aware of nonverbal communication; seeing potential threats everywhere.

The ride-along is a severe distraction, and another helpless person you're responsible for.

To make matters worse, they think they know everything and talk to everyone you meet. They never shut the hell up.

One night, a ride-along went out with one of the newer guys. The officer felt it was his duty to take the guy from one hot call to another.

They started out the shift hitting the first domestic that came in. A man and his wife had been drinking and fighting, and the man had beaten his wife up. The scene was secure, and by the time they arrived it was pretty much just a peep show, walking the ride-along through the scene and explaining what had happened.

The ride-along was disappointed; he wanted to see some "real action", not a cold domestic, but the situation was all cleaned up and the fighting was already over.

Next call was a DUI. The officer went to help out and stand by while the FSTs (field sobriety tests) were being done, and fill out the impound sheet for the suspect's car after it was towed.

This is the reality of cop work: boredom and paperwork, helping the other guy out, hoping to keep each other safe and prevent a situation from going bad and becoming a "CNN moment."

The ride-along complained that "this was boring" and he wanted to see some real action!!!

If it was me, he would have been out of the car at that point, walking his candy ass back to the police station, mumbling about what a prick I was as he passed the drunks and transients that frequented the area.

Police work isn't a ride in an amusement park; you pay a fee for fake thrills and the almost-danger of going fast on something that you have to be "this tall to ride."

This is the real deal, not a ride, and there's no safety inspector to warn you when things are getting ready to go to shit and ask you if you are sure you want to stay on the ride.

The night wore on with the cop trying to get his ride-along to more interesting calls, and the ride-along complaining that he was bored.

They were on another traffic stop that was a carload of gang bangers. They had stopped the car because it matched the description of a car involved in a drive by.

The incident had happened a few hours earlier, and they were checking out the occupants of the vehicle, getting identification on each and looking for weapons.

For the cops, it's a tense moment. Any traffic stop can go to shit in a moment, and that moment passes so fast, if you're not watching everything and seeing it almost before it happens, you end up breathing from new holes in your chest or face that aren't supposed to be there.

This stop was going well, and while they were identifying everyone, the ride-along sat in the car. Another unit stopped by, and they began to help out in the stop.

The cop had a weird feeling, he said later, and it turned out to be right.

The two officers re-approached the car and began to remove the occupants one at a time. Finally, they got down to just the driver and the right front passenger.

The officer that started the stop was talking to the driver, and the back up was on the passenger side, watching the front passenger.

While talking to the driver, the first cop was also watching the front passenger.

It's a reality of the job that you have to be aware of everything going on at all times; impossible task, but you try.

Anyway, while he was talking to the driver, the passenger looked back and saw the back up cop watching his every move.

What neither of the cops knew was that the carload of bangers had recently done a home burglary, and the trunk of the car was loaded up with rifles and handguns stolen in the burglary.

They had been driving around with the intention of "putting in work," meaning they were looking to get into a gunfight or do a drive-by on rival gang members, hoping to at least kill some rivals and make a name for the set. They were jacked up and angry, and looking for a fight—with anyone.

The passenger is watching the cop on his side, waiting for the cop to make a mistake, look away, lose his focus just for a second.

Finally, the moment came, and the back up looked down—just for a moment. The passenger took the opportunity and pulled a gun from his waist, twisting around almost 180 degrees in the front seat and pointing the gun at the back up officer, who was still looking down.

When the back up officer looked up, he was staring at the barrel of a stolen Glock 40 caliber handgun pointed at his face. The banger pulled the trigger.

Simultaneously, the primary officer was watching, and he pulled his gun and shot. He fired three rounds into the passenger while the driver was still sitting in the car, holding the steering wheel, gunpowder burning her face and eyes; the gun was that close when the shooting started.

She screamed and exits the car, running as fast as she could, screaming the entire way.

She was later located after people called the cops to report a hysterical screaming woman in the hallway of a nearby apartment building.

She was so traumatized by the shooting, she had a breakdown and just sat in the hallway, screaming and crying that her boyfriend had been killed.

Meanwhile, the banger had pulled the trigger on his Glock, trying to kill the back up cop.

He was a recent parolee from prison and wanted to die a hero to his set, and he figured that killing a cop was as good a way to go out as any; however, Karma—or whatever power you believe in—had different ideas.

The bullet did not fire, and the cop learned a valuable lesson the hard way and was able to survive that moment.

The banger was shot several times by the primary officer and eventually removed from the vehicle. He somehow survived the shooting and ended up back in prison. His hero status was intact; his life, however, was destroyed. He was nineteen years old.

His attempt to shoot the backup officer was confirmed by the firing pin striking deep on the primer of the unspent bullet found in the chamber of the Glock.

The bored ride-along? He was watching all of this. Again, Karma is a bitch; be careful what you wish for—especially on the street.

When the shooting broke out, the bored ride-along went from entertained amusement park rider wishing he had some popcorn and a drink while waiting for the next thrill from the safety of the front seat of the patrol car, to terrified dumbass, hoping to survive the next few moments.

Survival instinct has two options for any animal in life or death situations: fight or flight. The "I am bored, I want to see some action" reality show wannabe exited the vehicle as fast as his ass could go.

No longer concerned with the thrill of watching real cops in action, writing paperwork and going to cold calls, he was on the front row of a real battle for survival – and life or death battles are wicked, fast, and brutal.

He sat, jaw dropped and eyes wide open while the ejected brass from the cops' weapons bounced off the hood of the patrol car in front of him.

He exited the vehicle and ran as fast as he could, not caring where he went or what else happened; he just knew he had to get the fuck out of there—and now.

Later, after the scene was secured and medical arrived to treat the severely wounded gang member, the cop sent out word about the missing ride-along, and units were sent out to look for him.

After about twenty minutes of searching, the now not-so-bored ride-along was found about a half-mile away, walking in circles in a parking lot, sobbing and in shock.

He kept repeating, "I just want to go home" over and over.

After going through an interview and completing a written statement for investigators, he was released. He elected never to ride-along again...imagine that.

You Are In Or Out, No In-Between

COPS HAVE A WEIRD SENSE of who's in and who's out.

If you're in with one clique, you're usually out with another. I guess the old timers decided I was "OK" after I was in a couple of really messy calls.

They have a code that you have to have been baptized by fire before you're accepted by them. For the most part, this was cool with me.

I liked the old school cops as much as I liked the old school gang bangers. They all lived by a code; an old school unwritten code, but still a code. I understood that. I liked the way they treated each other. There was a sense of respect for who you were.

I was at the range, qualifying after the latest shit storm I'd survived. I was still a little shaken by it, and they put me back at the end of the qualification with the administration of the department.

I heard later that they did this in case I needed help qualifying, in case I'd lost my nerve. They didn't realize that I actually went the opposite direction.

I'd kept hidden from them some of the more serious incidents I've written about in the other books.

I wasn't about to lose my nerve; if anything, I was sharper than ever, too sharp. Edgy as hell.

So after I qualified, the administration was all gathered around, cleaning weapons and bragging about what they'd done back in the day when they were on the streets.

Funny thing about administration, they can't wait to get off the streets, feeling they're better than the rest of the street cops. Once they're off the streets, however, they can't seem to shut up about what "heroes" they were way back when. Legends in their own minds, I suppose.

I guess they felt like I belonged as well. They were trying hard to remember my name, patting me on the back while I cleaned my gun. I just wanted to get done and leave. The hair was standing up on the back of my neck.

I worked mid-shift to stay away from these guys. They weren't friends by any stretch of the imagination. They weren't the old school street cops; they were administration—and no one's friend.

So, while I was cleaning my gun, I overheard one asking the other to tell him about the guy above the river. They were all laughing about this.

Apparently, this is a story that was rarely told—and I'd soon know why.

As they whispered back and forth ("Do you think it's OK?", "Ya, he's OK; he won't mind"), I got the impression they were referring to me. I looked up, and they all looked at me; smiles from all these old dinosaurs as they looked my way. Yellow, old teeth; glassy blurry eyes... shit was creepy as fuck.

One of them started to tell a story about how he'd arrested this guy one night for being drunk at one of the bars in the city. He said that he was taking the guy to jail, then the guy started to talk trash to him in his car.

After a few well-placed insults about the cop's fat ass and potbelly, he was fed up and called another cop (who was now also sitting at the table at the range). They agreed to meet near the river that flowed through the center of the city.

They laughed as they recalled tying a rope to the suspect's feet and hanging him upside down from a large tree branch above the river.

They then bragged about shooting at him with rubber bullets numerous times as he hung helpless from the tree.

I stopped and looked down the table, listening at the laughing elderly men. I didn't laugh; I just stared quietly at them, one at a time. This shit was unreal.

These are the same two-faced dickwads that would hang one of us out to dry at the slightest hint of breaking one of the department's policies. They'd let guys go for not being able to pass the PT test after being injured on the job. They strutted around the department with this holier-than-thou attitude, barely able to recall your name when they said hello.

Here they are, bragging about a clear violation of the law—not to mention the guy's civil rights.

I listened while they bragged about letting the guy go after running out of rubber bullets. They took him to the county line and dropped him off, telling him never to return.

They then began to recall how they'd been pretty scared when the FBI showed up and began investigating the claims of a man being hung over the river and shot at by cops with rubber bullets. They laughed about how they'd defeated the investigation.

I shook my head and made eye contact with another guy who had missed his first appointment to qualify and had to shoot with them as well. His eyes were wide in amazement, and he said under his breath, "Can you believe this shit?"

I replied, also in a whisper, "Ya! I can."

I finished cleaning my gun and began to leave the range. They called to me again—using the wrong name—saying, "Where you going? Hey, come back and sit with us."

I didn't reply; I just got into my car and left.

The next time I saw one of them in the hallway at work, the nonverbal communication was clear. Old eyes glaring at me now disapprovingly; I wasn't to be trusted, I wasn't one of them—and they now knew that. I was definitely out.

14 The Witches Of Central City

AFTER YOU'RE ON THE STREET for a while, you get less and less excited about the calls. Your imagination is less involved, and reality is more what you gauge the threat and the intensity of the call by.

I went to a house on a report from an older woman that her schizophrenic daughter had become too difficult to manage.

The people in the neighborhoods of central city thought of the two women as witches. They were given a lot of room by the central city dwellers for fear that a curse or some other black arts magic might be thrown their way should they cross the witches.

Reality, however, was that both women lived very sad, lonely lives, struggling with mental illness and a lack of any real, healthy contact with their fellow city dwellers.

I arrived, and the mother said that her daughter had been off her medication since she broke up with her latest boyfriend.

He'd left when the schizophrenic illness became too much to tolerate, and she was devastated. Going upstairs to meet with the daughter, I heard her screaming out incoherently. She was definitely off her medication.

I had Jeff with me on one of his last days as a reserve on the department. He'd tested and made the list on several police departments, and he wanted to work in St. Pauls, but he'd been picked up by another larger department. It would be a great thing for him; not so much for me.

I opened the door, and we went into the daughter's bedroom. She was as feral as I'd ever seen her. The illness was in full swing, and she was in bad shape: raving, drooling, and screaming—clawing at the air one moment and crying and whimpering the next. It was a sad thing to see.

I tried to talk her into coming with me, and she lunged at me, stopping inches from my face and screaming at an all-out blood curdling volume that should have made me jump.

By this time, not much phased me, so I looked back at her and told her to get her shoes on; she needed help, and we both knew it.

She glared at me for a while, then a small glimmer of who she was came through her eyes; it was a small moment of recognition. "Slick? Is that you?" this little child-like voice said.

I said, "Yes, it's me. Will you come with me?"

She said yes and started to cry. She told me about her latest boyfriend leaving and that she felt that she wanted to die. She looked at me and said, "If I died, would you care, Slick?"

I said, "Of course, I would care."

I told her I was here to help her. I could just leave and say her mother was crazy as well and not take her to get help, but I wouldn't do that; I wanted her to get help.

She smiled, then said, "Thank you, Slick."

As she started to get ready, I turned to Jeff and could see he was still amazed by the war cry she'd let loose just inches from my face. His adrenaline was pumping.

We talked later, and I told him that I'd dealt with many mentally ill people in the area. I found that most were manageable and were nothing to be afraid of—as long as they weren't armed. Had she been armed, this call might have gone a lot differently.

He smiled and said, "Sure, whatever!"

I took the daughter to the hospital and stayed with her during the intake process. She was singing a song that I recognized, and as she did, she started to get jacked up again, repeating the lyrics over and over, louder and louder.

The nurses and ER staff were becoming anxious and afraid.

I recognized the song; it was Bruce Dickenson's latest album at the time, Balls to Picaso. The song was "Tears of the Dragon."

When she stopped to catch her breath (after nearly screaming the lyrics out), I quietly repeated the next verse, and she stopped screaming, startled that I knew the lyrics.

She smiled and said, "You like that song?" in a quiet, little girl voice again. I said that I did.

She said, "Me, too; it makes me feel normal."

The ER nurse looked at me, surprised at the rapport that I had with the younger "witch."

It was really sad to see how tortured the young girl was by the illness and how hard she struggled to have some kind of happiness in her life.

As I was leaving, the nurse said, "You sure have a way with the crazies, Slick."

Another one of the last calls with Jeff was a report of three men fighting in a garage on the east side. I cancelled the back up since it was Skidmark and I had Jeff with me.

Jeff said, "Are you sure that's a good idea, Zach? I'm just a reserve, and there are three of them—and they're fighting."

I told him, "Ya, I'd cancel Skidmark anyway—even if you weren't here. With you here, the odds are better than normal."

On the way, we received more information from the complainant that the three men were definitely fighting. They were yelling and swearing, and the complainant heard one of them say, "How you like that, motherfucker?" after a loud crash came from the garage.

Jeff was getting really jacked up. He was breathing hard already in anticipation of the battle he was sure we'd be fighting in a few moments.

I kept telling him that this was a bad idea, to arrive with an idea in mind of how the call would be.

I'd learned the hard way over and over again not to get caught up in the call and let emotion run my decision-making.

We arrived blacked out and coasted to a stop, parking down the street from the address we were given.

As soon as we got out of the car, we could hear the men's voices—and they were very loud.

I tried to calm Jeff down, but I could tell it was too late; he was in survival mode already, terrified of the battle he knew we were about to be in.

We walked up to the house and carefully looked around the corner to the detached garage.

There was a loud crash, and then someone said, "That's what I'm talking about, motherfucker!" and then "What? What?"

There was something familiar in that voice.

I stepped out and walked up to the garage, looking through the crack in the door.

The three guys inside were playing dominoes and slamming the tiles on the table where they were playing.

I recognized them immediately as the mall security guards I mentioned in *StreetCreds*. They were drinking Old English 800 beer and playing a very enthusiastic game of dominoes.

I called Jeff over and had him look in on the "fight."

He watched, and I could tell from his body language that he began to calm down immediately. He looked at me and rolled his eyes. "How did you know?" he whispered.

I didn't know anything; I'd just finally learned not to get caught up in the call. It only took me fifteen years or more,—I was a slow learner!

We opened the door and started talking to Riggins and Pogar and another guy I didn't know. I told them about the report of a fight, and they all busted out laughing.

They said, "Are you serious?" I told them I wouldn't be there otherwise.

I left after they promised to bring it down a notch or two, and we walked back to the car.

Jeff was still shaking from the adrenaline dumps. Dominoes can be intense like that.

15 Dreaming About Lassie The Land Shark

BEING IN K-9 HAD BEEN a dream for me for years.

I went into the military with the promise from the recruiter that I'd be assigned to K-9 once I completed Basic.

Like most 18-year-old kids looking at the contract to sign up for military service, I had no idea what the language meant. I trusted the guy (foolishly), and when I arrived I found out I'd never be allowed to be in K-9. I was in the wrong career field.

I was really pissed, and when I completed the training for Basic and tech school, I came back to find the recruiter. He was gone, of course, moved on to another assignment; meanwhile, I'm in a career where I get to watch K-9 handlers almost daily—but never actually handle the dog.

It was like being a fat kid in a bakery with no money; it drove me crazy. Eventually, I found the SAC combat competition and poured my frustration into that.

After I got out of the military and became a civilian cop, I was like a heat-seeking missile on the K-9 program.

I read everything I could read about training dogs. I talked to the old handlers and picked their brains about different techniques and practices.

A lot of what you read is theory; reality is a whole other thing.

It takes an amazing dog to be K-9. They're like world-class athletes, combined with the instincts of a MMA fighter and the intellect of a Nobel Peace Prize winner. Imagine Mike Tyson, Usain Bolt, and Albert Einstein rolled into one man. That's your *average* police dog! They're truly amazing.

The K-9 handler has to be pretty amazing, as well.

Picture being able to understand your spouse or best friend completely by their body language. Seeing their moods, feelings, and understanding exactly how they felt that day by the way they held their shoulders or ears or the eye contact they made.

It's an amazing talent to be a dog handler, and I truly believe that they're as rare as the dogs themselves.

When the Sergeant in charge of K-9 retired, we had an opening. The political powers had decided that increasing the K-9 unit was a good idea and decided to do just that.

I applied for a position in K-9 and was the number one selectee in my department.

The process was meant to weed out those who were just in it for the alleged glory of the position.

The job is incredibly challenging; you always have the dog with you, caring for it, training it, and socializing it so that you can have it in public in a large crowd without incident—but given the correct command, Lassie becomes a land shark! All teeth and attitude, ready to take out whoever you direct the dog to attack.

It's quite an accomplishment to take an animal as intelligent and driven as a police dog and form the team that makes the K-9 unit.

I thought I was up to the challenge...I wasn't.

A dog handler has to be patient beyond belief. They literally have to be able to project themselves into the dog's head and see what the dog sees, smells, hears, and sometimes fears.

They have to read all that in the body language of the animal. No words pass between them that don't come from the handler. They not only speak different languages, they're entirely different species. That's the reality of K-9.

I was assigned EMO, a sleek, black athletic dog fresh from the newly reunited country of Germany.

He was from the former East German side of the country and only "spoke" German; so, not only did I have to learn "dog language", now I had to learn German to speak his human commands.

No biggie, I thought, I'll learn German and "Dog", and he'll love me and follow me wherever I go, my loyal and amazing dog. My dream had finally come true.

Wrong! I was book smart; I knew everything I could read about dogs after eight years of watching from the outside, and finally I was in.

I failed as a K-9 handler miserably.

EMO was gifted. He had a nose like no other dog I'd ever seen. He could find one damn pot seed in a house within a few seconds and let me know it was there instantly by his body language.

I was able to read him pretty well after a while. He was an amazing dog when it came to dope. He loved it.

He had a prey drive that was amazingly high, "prey" being the desire of the dog to hunt. Cats, skunks, raccoons, dope—we trained the dogs to think of the dope as prey, and they'd hunt for the dope like they'd hunt in the wild for an animal.

EMO was the idiot savant of dope.

When the Narcotics strike force called me to do a search of a house, I knew immediately when I arrived at the door if there was dope in the house. Didn't matter where it was hidden or how it had been disguised, he smelled it and found it.

He seriously found a single pot seed in a heater vent after searching the entire house during one search.

I took the vent out, expecting him to have found a large stash; there was nothing. I looked and looked; I could find nothing. I brought him back to the vent, and EMO told me, "Dude, it's in there; I swear to God, it's there."

By this time, I knew to trust his nose, so I kept at it—and finally I noticed the round seed in the round tin heating duct and removed it. Holding it up, I thought, *Jesus, really? You can smell this?*

I had him check again, and the body language was "Nothing here; can we go now?"

I was amazed and proud of the piece of trash. (All K-9 handlers referred to their dogs as "trash"; it's meant as a term of endearment and respect. You realize early on how special the dogs really are).

EMO loved dope, but he was one moody ass dog.

He was dual certified, meaning he could do dope (which he loved) or he could do apprehension (which he tolerated).

He loved to search buildings and could fight if he had to protect me (if he decided to that day).

Here's an example of an average day with EMO:

I received a call to search a building that had been broken into.

Patrol had responded to an alarm and found the building open. One of the doors had been pried open with a crowbar, and the silent alarm had gone off. They'd set up a perimeter and felt there was a good possibility that the burglar was still inside.

I got EMO out, and he was his usual happy self (hoping to search for dope, I'm sure); however, when I made it to the door and told him to drop while I yelled out the standard warning (that I was the K-9 unit and we were going to search with a dog, come out now and you won't be hurt), EMO's body language changed.

If he was speaking my language, he would have said, "Man, I hate this shit. I really do. I thought we were gonna play dope."

Anyway, I did the call out and encouraged him, praising him and getting him jacked up and ready to search.

Then I gave him the command to search.

He started off fast, then about ten feet in he stopped, turned around, and stared at me as his ears went back.

Head up, chest out, his ears came back up, then he started to walk towards me; he was challenging me.

In a K-9 handler and dog relationship, the handler has to been seen as the Alpha dog. They're a pack, a unit, and the handler has to be—without question—the leader. In every pack there's a leader, and there are the dogs that challenge the leader.

EMO, being the moody ass that he was, challenged me constantly.

He was rank as hell, meaning he always felt that he should be Alpha dog and I should be doing what he wanted. He didn't like being told to do anything.

So, he was challenging me for Alpha dog right here in the middle of the search.

I said out loud, "Seriously, motherfucker? Right now?"

He growled and showed me his teeth, and my back up said, "Who are you talking to?"

I said, "Back out; the dog wants to fight."

He said, "What the fuck?"

I said, "Back out now!"

He backed out as EMO came for me.

I caught him in mid-air, snapping and growling, then rolled him into a subordinate position called an Alpha roll.

An Alpha roll forces the dog on his back, exposed to you, while you're over him, dominating him and looking into his eyes, showing your superiority and staring him down.

He'd challenged me this way many times, but never in a search.

EMO was growling and digging with his paws, trying to bite me. The backup officer was stunned, and I heard him say behind me, "Holy fuck—your dog is crazy."

After about five minutes, EMO submitted; satisfied that I'd earned the Alpha dog status, he relaxed and looked away.

As his body loosened, I let him up, then put him back in a ready position and called out the warning again.

He was on now, ready to do what I asked.

I gave the command to search, and away he went.

When I entered the building, my back up wouldn't come in.

He said, "Fuck you! That dog is fucking crazy; you're on your own."

Great news! Now I was searching the entire building without a back up.

EMO found nothing inside; whoever was in the building had escaped before the perimeter was set up by patrol.

He came out happy and playful while I praised him for his work. He was back!

"EMO the wonder dog" was always a challenge. The patrol unit, on the other hand, thought we were both nuts.

Since then, I've heard from many handlers that the dog always reflects the handler. Maybe that's true; I don't know.

I was a pain in the ass as well, always defying the brass and doing what I thought was best, in spite of what the "rule book" said.

We had many adventures, EMO and I, and I admit now that we were more alike than I cared to believe at the time.

16 It's A Bird, It's A Plane, It's Emo The Wonder Dog

ANOTHER IN-PROGRESS CALL AND ANOTHER search with EMO, the wonder dog.

Residents had called to report a burglary in progress at a house in their neighborhood. The neighborhood was well off, and the house was owned by some very wealthy people who had been on vacation. They'd asked a neighbor to watch the house, who said they'd been watching as a man had arrived and entered the house.

They were positive he'd broken in, and when I arrived, they told me that they believed he was still inside.

Again, I had no back up. We were short on personnel and had no available units.

This is the reality of police work. You try to be as safe as possible, but sometimes you have to enter a situation that can't be made safe.

Critics will tell you that you always have the choice; no shit, we all know that—but like EMO the wonder dog wanting to be the Alpha, cops are the Alpha dogs as well. We don't wanna bow down to anyone. Out numbered and out gunned, we still run *towards* the shooting when common sense would say to run the other fucking direction.

Don't ask me why that is; I don't know. I just know that for me to walk away from a fight, a real fight—especially where someone else might die if I don't get involved—is almost impossible. Criticize it all you want; it's who I am.

So anyway, EMO and I were at the open door left by the burglar. I put him in a down position and did the call out. I checked EMO's body language, and today he was on. He was going to search. I gave the command, and away he went. We were off searching.

One of the things about a rank dog that's really cool is that they're independent. EMO never needed my reassurance; he was positive that he was the toughest, baddest land shark on the planet.

Both he and I searched, me with my gun out. We crossed paths many times, me watching his body language as he searched.

I trusted his nose, and he was wind scenting, nose up high, checking the air currents in the house. His body language said, "No one is home, but I smell something."

I checked the house and found nothing.

EMO wasn't done yet, however; he was still searching, and his body language told me he was in prey mode, not fight mode.

Had he found some dope? I couldn't tell, so I watched…then out of nowhere, a cat bolted across the living room floor in front of us. Scared the shit out of me.

EMO was like a heat-seeking missile and chased the hated, evil cat.

Animal rights folks won't like this, but I'd learned by this time that EMO had a prey drive (a desire to hunt) that was uncontrollable. Two skunks and a raccoon later, I'd bought an electric shock collar to keep him in check, and he wore it daily. He had it on now, and I had the controller on my duty belt.

To keep him in check, it had to be on the highest setting. (That setting would send another dog into total submission, begging the handler to stop; EMO, on the other hand, was like me: stupid stubborn and crazy determined. When either one of us were in the hunt, there was no stopping us—short of killing us.)

He was after the cat, and I gave him the command in German to stop and lie down.

He heard nothing; there was a cat in the house—and for him, this was better than sex. Hunting was his sole reason to live.

The cat ran around the room, barely evading the pursing land shark, which was snapping, and growling.

I lit him up with the electric collar three times, and his body would contort from the electrical current running through his neck, but he wouldn't slow down in his pursuit of the hated cat. I was sure the cat was dead.

The owners had left a sliding glass door open and the screen locked. The cat ran right through the screen at full speed, punching a small hole in its fabric. We were on the third floor of the huge home, and the sliding glass door led to a balcony that surrounded the house. EMO hit the door a second later, taking the entire screen door out. I was right behind them, hoping to save the cat.

They circled the house once on the balcony. I lit EMO up twice more, and he barely reacted to the shock. He could sense the kill was within his grasp, and he'd finally have the wily cat!

The cat had other ideas. It was desperate and finally took the only out left: it hit the only chair on the balcony, then the ledge surrounding the balcony, and launched into the air.

Three stories up, the cat was flying, airborne.

EMO was about a half-second behind and hit the chair, then the balcony ledge as well.

His ears flopped in the wind for a moment, then I think he finally realized what the cat had done: it had drawn him in, then launched off the balcony. It was maybe six pounds and would probably survive the fall; EMO was ninety-five pounds.

I stopped at the balcony and he turned his head and looked at me as he fell.

For the very first time, I saw EMO the puppy; he was scared and had the "Oh shit! Help me, Dad!" look on his face.

About a second later, the cat hit ground and was off running. It had survived the gamble and was headed to the nearest tree as fast as it could go.

I didn't wait to see how EMO landed.

I was sure he'd have broken legs, at the very least, after he hit the ground. I was hoping that he'd just survive the fall.

I was running through the house, imagining him with broken legs and shattered teeth, lying in the driveway, whimpering.

I opened the door, and there he was, meekly wagging his tail. He was humbled for the first and only time I ever saw the entire time that I worked with him.

He hit hard enough to knock loose his pride, but that was all. He had a small cut on his chin, his teeth were all in good shape, and he had no broken bones. I was relieved he was OK.

Maybe I'm reading into it, but the way I read his body language was this: "I almost had him, Dad—did you see that? I almost had him!"

I told him to go to the truck, and off he went, head down, tail wagging low and slowly. The electric collar, scarred up from the impact after the jump, hung uselessly around his neck. We never found the burglar. He'd left long before we arrived, frightened off by the neighbors.

Looking back now, I think the old handlers were more on the mark than I ever realized. EMO and I had a lot more in common than I'd ever admit. We were both hard-headed, determined, and had our own agenda. To hell with what others thought about us; we did what we wanted to do, even to our own detriment. We both resented the hell out of authority, and we both loved intense physical activity.

I'd take him running, and he was my best bud. He loved to work out. Like me, he didn't like to fight and only did it if he had to—but when he had to, it was a thing of beauty.

The sleek, solid black dog closing on a bad guy trying to run away, trying to do the impossible and escape EMO and his amazing nose... that was a sight that only a dog handler can appreciate. EMO launching his body and hitting the guy, knocking him to the ground, and then biting if the guy continued to resist.

For some reason, he'd spit out a suspect as soon as I gave the command and back off, ready to attack again if I gave the command.

I know for a fact that if he ever caught that cat, there would be no spitting him out 'til EMO was satisfied he was dead. The cat, the hunt; that was his passion. The suspect? That was just work.

17 Never Judge A Book By Its Cover

I WAS WORKING ONE NIGHT, and a guy came to me and asked me to take a ride-along. I rolled my eyes. *Jesus, really?*

He said, "I know you don't like them, but I told her she could ride along, and I forgot that I'd already told another guy he could come out. I can't take both."

Some guys were like that; they loved showing off the cop skills they thought they had.

Like I said before, I hated ride-alongs.

I said, "Look, man, you know how I feel about ride-alongs; if she gets in my car and starts talking nonstop, her ass is out on the curb."

He replied, "I know, I know. You know she won't last long—but I promised, so just make it look good, then kick her out so I won't get in trouble."

I agreed to take the ride-along. As I walked back in to the police station, he said, "Oh! She's a college ride-along, a Criminal Justice major."

He then ran off laughing, knowing I was in for a very long couple hours until I could get her out of the car.

I walked into the station and went to the lobby. I looked around for the college kid, imagining the pimple-faced fat girl wanting to someday be a cop and cure the world of all that was wrong.

I could see the image in my mind: chewing gum, greasy hair, glasses. We'd start off with her telling me she knew all about police work and that she was Soooo excited. "Like, oh my God!" The acid was already pouring into my guts at the aggravation; fuck, I did *not* want to do this.

I looked in the lobby and saw no one resembling a college student. Several people were there, waiting for copies of reports or wanting to talk to the night detectives.

I went to the desk Sergeant who was dealing with the crowd and said, "Hey, Sgt., I'm supposed to meet a ride-along. Has anyone come in?"

He said, "Ya, one woman was here asking about that."

I turned around, and there was the woman he was referring to.

When I was at work, people registered with me mentally by threat. I'd looked at the woman and not even registered that she was there. She was dressed in business attire, not casually. She was *not* a college kid; instead, she was in her mid-twenties.

I said, "Are you supposed to ride tonight?" Still not sure that this was correct.

She smiled and said, "Yes." She then stood up and introduced herself.

I said, "OK, well we're outside and I have a call pending already, so we have to go."

Time to start this off on the right foot and make sure that she knew I wasn't going to be friendly.

We walked to the car, and I got in. She walked to the other side. We hadn't talked at all on the way to the car. I was already counting down the minutes 'til she'd fake a headache or stomach cramps to get the hell out of my car.

I'd noticed that most of the female ride-alongs liked to be coddled; flirt with them, and they'll never go away—so I was a royal asshole.

I backed out of the parking lot and was all business on the way to the call, with waves of hostility rolling off me. She didn't say a word.

When we arrived, I said bluntly, "Don't talk to anyone, don't answer questions; you get out and stay near me...you watch and observe. One comment about anything you've learned in school, and you're back at the station as fast as I can get you there. We clear?"

She said, "Yes, clear."

We got out and made it through the entire call without her saying one word.

I was disappointed, hoping for an excuse to get rid of her. I wrote reports in silence, and then went on to the next call.

Three calls later, we were at one of the houses of a Peewee gang member. His mom and her boyfriend had been drunk, and the mom wanted him out of the house for the night. They'd been in a pretty big fight. Neighbors were involved, and there were a lot of witnesses. It was a strange scene.

Everyone we talked to kept looking at the ride-along, staring at her.

I was frustrated.; she hadn't asked to go back to the station yet, and the two-hour mark was getting near. I was being a complete ass, and nothing was working.

To make matters worse, I couldn't get anyone—men or women—to stay focused on the questions I asked. They'd start to answer, then turn to look at the ride-along, watching her.

To her credit, one guy started to talk to her, assuming she was a detective; that's how professionally she was dressed. She told him that he'd have to speak to me only and said nothing else.

We got back in the car afterward, and I said, "Do you know them?" She said, "No."

I said, "Weird that everyone is staring at you."

We went on to the next call, and then the next. Finally, I said, "Do you wanna get a drink? Need to use the restroom?" She said, "Sure, if that's what you'd like to do."

This was weird; nothing like the usual ride-alongs asking to be pampered and coddled, talking to everyone at the scenes we went to, changing the radio station, adjusting the heater. She was quiet and respectful.

I went to the usual place I went to get a drink, checking the store before I entered to make sure that it wasn't being robbed. The area I worked was tough, and the store had been robbed many times at gunpoint.

I got out again, ignoring her, and entered the store.

I hit the restroom, then got a drink. While I was paying, I noticed the clerk watching her as well. She was looking at drinks, trying to decide what to get. He was fixed on her, staring.

I said, "Hey, man, can I get my drink?"

He said, "Oh ya, sure, brotha. Who is that?"

I said, "A ride-along."

He said, "Oh."

I asked, "Why?"

He said, "Jesus, she's beautiful."

I said, "Huh? Really?"

I hadn't even really looked at her, I was too busy focusing on the problem of getting her out of the car as soon as possible. I went out to the car and thought that was weird. I waited while she got her stuff, paid, then walked to the car.

The night wore on, and she never left; no matter how I tried to be an ass, she was still there. At the end of the shift, I took her to the station and dropped her off at the car, then she asked if I'd mind if she rode with me again. I thought it over.

She *had* been really quiet, and she hadn't asked any stupid questions. I guess it would be OK.

I said, "Yes, you can ride again—on one condition." Her eyes glazed over, her face became hardened, and her tone changed.

She said, "What's that?"

I said, "You're gonna have to change the way you dress. I work the worst area in the city, and you stick out like a sore thumb. Everyone was staring at you all night. If you're gonna ride with me, you're gonna have to fit in this area. You're too dressed up. Simple shit, really. If you wanna ride with me, those are my rules."

She was stunned. She stared at me and said quietly, "That's it?"

"Ya, that's it," I said. *Jesus, this is police work—not a business meeting.*

She relaxed and said, "What should I wear, then?"

I replied, "Really? I have to explain this? Wear some fuckin' Levis, a jacket, ball cap, and running shoes. Not slacks and pumps and a business jacket."

She stared at me in disbelief.

I looked back and said, "I'm serious! You come back dressed like that, and you're not going with me."

She agreed and asked if she could ride the next week.

I said, "Sure."

The entire time she was in the ride-along program, she ended up riding with me and turned out to be a real asset on several calls. She was quiet and smart, and she was the first ride-along I actually thought might be able to become a good cop.

18 Clean Up On Aisle 5

SUMMERTIME IS A BUSY TIME for cops. Kids are out of school, so juvenile crimes skyrocket.

In spite of what Daywalkers think, it isn't the hardened career criminals that make up the majority of our work; juvenile crime accounts for a huge percentage of the crime we deal with.

Summer also brings out the tourists, feeling they're entitled to special treatment because they're spending their money in "your city," demanding to be let go for whatever crime they've committed—or they'll never spend another penny of their money in this city again!

Summer also brings out my personal favorite: the transients.

Yep, summer keeps us cops hopping.

There's another downside of summer, as well, and that's the heat—but not in a way that you'd understand unless you were a cop.

I got a call in a large apartment complex in central city one night. The tenants weren't prone to calling us at all. It was the inner city; cops weren't welcome until the shit really hit the fan—and then it was a love-hate relationship: you were welcomed only for the moment.

"Please deal with this shit storm we've called you to fix, then please leave as fast as you came."

Anyway, the occupants lived in pretty bleak conditions. People pissed in the stairwells and left their garbage in the hallways for someone else to put out for the trash. The place smelled pretty bad on a daily basis, and in the summer the stench was horrendous.

When tenants called one day and complained about the smell coming from a specific apartment, I knew this would be a call I wish I never received.

I arrived at the apartment complex and was met in the parking lot by the man who called. Word had gone out through the hallways that the cops were on their way, and as I arrived cars were leaving the parking lot and people were suddenly remembering their New Year's resolutions to start exercising more. (Keep in mind, it's July now). There was a mass exodus from the building.

The caller said that there was something wrong in a third story apartment. An older woman rented the apartment, and she was always very quiet. He said no one had seen her in about two weeks and that now there was an odd odor in the hallway around her place. He was worried something bad had happened. He said he'd knocked several times, but no one answered.

I sighed heavily, then opened my trunk and pulled out some Vicks vapor rub that I kept for just such calls. This was really gonna suck. I dabbed the vapor rub on my upper lip and said to the man, "OK, show me where she lives."

The manager had arrived as I was getting the information from the caller, and I offered them both a bit of the Vicks. They looked at me strangely, exchanging odd glances, then politely refused the offer and rolled their eyes at the peculiar cop that had arrived.

We entered the building and headed up the stairs, and by the second floor I could smell the familiar odor.

By the time we reached the apartment door, I swear you could see the odor in the air. In my mind, the colors were a dark brown, black, and green swirling in the air, thick and toxic.

"Last chance for the Vicks." I said as I offered it to the manager and caller.

They were gagging and coughing, but said no.

The manager opened the door, and the stench of the most disgusting smells you can imagine being thrown in your face hit us like a wet curtain.

Both the manager and the caller threw up right there—several times—and I stepped aside to keep the mess off my clothes and shoes.

I went into the apartment and searched for the dead body I knew I'd find inside. I found the elderly woman lying on the floor of her bathroom, dead, naked, and lying in a pool of her own bodily fluids.

Her body had blown up like a balloon from the gases of decomposing flesh. Eventually, the body started to seep out fluid on the floor, and she was lying in that. I saw no signs that she'd died anything but a natural death at home, but in the cop world you have to prove that.

Detectives were called, as well as CSI. The scene was processed, the body eventually removed, and after a while your senses started to dull to the overwhelming stench.

The vapor rub helped dull the sense of smell. It is an old cop trick to use either vapor rub or a smoking cigar on dead body scenes.

I don't know if it's psychological or what, but after every dead body call I can never seem to get the smell out of my clothes, hair, and literally the taste out of my mouth.

I was late getting home that morning, and I went right to the bathroom, stripped, and started to brush my teeth. I put my uniform in the washing machine, then took a shower, scrubbing my face and the inside of my nose to try to get the smell out.

After washing my face half a dozen times, cutting the hair out of my nose, and shaving my moustache, the smell started to go away. It was disgusting.

The next day in briefing, Sergeant Duke asked me about the change in my facial hair. I told him that I couldn't get the woman's decomposing smell off me, so I shaved. He laughed; everyone did. We'd all been there at one time or another.

Dead bodies are the calls we all hated and never talked about.

He began to tell us a story that had occurred to him in his first couple years of being in the department.

He said one of the first dead bodies he'd been on as a younger cop was a very large woman who had died and fallen on the kitchen floor. She was wearing a housedress, at least, and wasn't naked when they arrived.

She lay there for a couple days 'til the smell reached the neighbor's house and they called. He said that he and another officer had been assigned the call, and when they arrived they did the routine investigative tasks and eventually called a mortuary to come pick up the body.

The morticians arrived with a gurney and placed it next to the body for a quick pick up. They stood at the head of the body, and because the woman was really large, they asked the two young cops to take her feet.

Duke said he should have known something was wrong, but he was young in his time on the force. He still believed people were basically good and meant you no ill will as a cop.

They counted to three, agreeing to lift the woman on three. Each man grabbed a limb: the two morticians grabbed the arms, and the two younger cops grabbed each of the legs.

On three, they all lifted.

Duke said that just before they lifted the woman, he noticed the dead woman was wearing no underwear (we all grimaced); it was about to get a lot worse.

Duke said instantly he and the other cop were sprayed in the face and chest with bodily fluids that came shooting out of the dead woman's vagina and anus.

He said she'd blown up with gases from the decomposing flesh and was like a balloon waiting to pop; when they lifted her, that's exactly what she did: "pop."

He said they each received a face full of the spraying fluids and dropped the body instantly—and the body hit the floor and sprayed all over them again.

We were all in tears, laughing as we sat and listened to the story. This was the single most horrible account of a dead body call that we'd ever heard.

He looked at me as he laughed and said, "Remember that no matter how bad it is, it could always—and I mean *always*—be a lot worse."

Duke always had a way of making the worst things we went through seem manageable and survivable, making us all share in the horrors of the street in a way that could make us laugh about the worst of what we had to do.

We laughed hard about this story and asked questions, laughing at his account of what happened next. It was an incredibly funny, disgusting story.

He said after that, he always made sure that if he picked up any dead body, he *always* had an arm.

19

The Low Down
On The Low Down

CENTRAL CITY WAS A STRANGE collection point for the area.

For some reason, it seemed like everything came back to central city. All the crime, all the dark and hidden undercurrents of the area came back to the toilet bowl we called central city.

One early morning, I was patrolling the area; the city had finally fallen asleep, and the morning was slowly starting to brighten the horizon. Black changed slowly to dark blue, then lightened up and started to wake up the brighter side of the city, loosening the grip the night held on it.

It was the only peaceful time I ever saw in the city, a brief period between night and day where the dark and evil side retreated and the Daywalkers weren't awake yet.

I was winding down from a night of battles, double-checking businesses to make sure they were still secure and that there was nothing obvious that I'd missed during the night.

On this early morning, a call came in from an address I'd never visited. It was some type of business that was housed in a renovated older home right at the center of my area. It was an exception to the rule of my area.

The home was immaculate, the yard and shrubs perfect. There was a sign in the front yard that had the business name and logo, but no indication of what work they actually did inside.

Anyway, someone from inside the business called to report that someone was breaking in. We took calls like that often that turned out to be nothing. I went anyway to check it out.

When I was halfway to the call, the occupant called back, scared and screaming that the burglar was inside the business. The caller had grabbed the cordless phone and locked themself inside the bathroom, staying on the line with our dispatchers.

I picked it up, pushing the patrol car to its limits and arriving a few seconds later. I told the dispatcher to let the caller know that I was at the scene and to stay in the bathroom.

I saw that the front door to the business had a large oval decorative glass piece that had been shattered; the call was legit.

I drew my Glock and carefully walked through the broken glass, ready to fight it out with whoever had broken into the business. I searched the building quickly and found nothing, no one.

My back up arrived, and we did a more thorough search. We found a guy hiding in a utility closet on the main floor. He was covered in sweat and terrified.

After a few tense moments of talking him out of the closet at gunpoint, we placed him under arrest.

After a couple moments of conversation, it was plain to see that the guy was tweekin': suffering from the side effects of meth and several days without sleep.

He'd been hallucinating and thought that he was being shot at by several people with AK-47s and chased by pit bulls. He'd broken into the business as a last gasp attempt to escape the crazed killers he was sure were still just outside, waiting to kill him. He was almost as happy to see us as the worker at the business who was still locked in the bathroom, on the phone with our dispatch.

Once we made sure the rest of the house was secure and no other tweekers were inside the business, we coaxed the worker out of the bathroom, and I began to collect her information for the report.

Nothing had been taken, and the tweeker had harmed no one; he just wanted to survive his imagined attackers.

After I transported him to jail, I returned to the business and asked the worker what they did there. I'd worked the area for many years and always wondered what they did, but I was always too busy to think about stopping to ask what went on there.

It looked like a doctor's or lawyer's office; however, I noticed the lights were on twenty-four hours a day, and I never saw anyone ever enter or exit the business.

The worker felt indebted, I guess; I seriously doubt that I ever would have found out the true purpose of the business if I'd just stopped and asked.

The frightened worker was a woman in her early thirties. She said to me, "Are you sure you really want to know what we do here?" I said yes.

It always helped to understand what was going on in the area on many levels. Each layer I uncovered explained to me more in depth why what happened did happen, and the "why" was always important to me. Understanding the layers of the city and how they fit and affected each other could make the obscure and apparently unrelated events suddenly all fall into place.

Imagine a huge, complex Rubik's cube or puzzle that had many levels hidden below the facade you saw on the surface; the only way to solve crimes and make a difference in the area was to understand the puzzle on multiple levels.

Did I want to know what she did in the business? Definitely!

Another layer of the puzzle, another piece was about become clearer.

She explained that the company was a messaging service. They were a place for the elite businessmen and women of the area to have their messages collected and sent to them while they were at home or at work.

They were very discreet, and because of that they'd earned a reputation with the wealthy business people in the area as a company that could be trusted with their secrets; personal and business secrets.

They kept files on who called their clients so that the "operator" was able keep the secret lives of their clients separate from their professional lives.

Basically, it worked like this: doctors, lawyers, and business men and women would have families with the spouse or partner that had gotten them to the position they were in. This was their surface life, the life the public saw.

On the "down low", they had sexual partners of both sexes that they spent time with on the side, and they'd use the service to keep their two lives separated. They'd give the men or women in both lives the service's phone number. It was a way to contact them.

It was the "operator's" job to keep track of where the client really was, as well as what the cover story was that they'd told the person who wanted to leave a message for their client; basically, they kept track of the lie, maintaining the façade for their client.

The Daywalker side of the city would never tolerate this kind of behavior, so they kept it hidden and on the "down low"; maintaining lovers on the side in addition to the spouses and families would be severely frowned upon by the business communities and religious culture that dominated the area.

I was fascinated. I'd come across this facet of the city a few times during my travels in and out of the many hidden layers of deceit that shrouded the city. Here was a focal point where the rich all came together with their dirty little secrets.

She showed me a room full of file cabinets that housed their clients' files. She said if the information in those files was made public... WOW! The local churches, government, and businesses would never be the same.

I laughed. We both laughed hard.

We both knew the secrets that the people in the city held close, living their double lives. This was a hidden secret that the elite kept among themselves.

The poor had their own secrets to keep, and the similarities of the two social classes were always so amazing to me.

I started to stop in occasionally and talk to the woman, picking her brain about incidents that happened in the city and surrounding areas. We started to develop trust in each other.

She could often fill in the blanks on many incidents that didn't fit or make sense: how certain people were selected for certain positions in government; elected officials who granted building zoning changes in certain areas in the city; doctors and lawyers that would be entangled in weird, messy incidents that made no sense on the surface.

All the stories would suddenly be made crystal clear when I knew the background provided by the woman. If I had been an investigative reporter instead of a cop, the local paper would have increased its subscription rate dramatically.

We shared many secrets, each of us filling in the blanks that occurred in the stories that went on in the city. The down low was always incredibly fascinating.

Best Friends For Life

JIM HAYES AND LARRY FOWLER were best friends. They'd gone to high school together, played high school sports together, and even been the best man at each other's weddings. They had a close relationship, and when Jim was going through a divorce, Larry stayed at his house for a couple days to help him get through it.

Jim had caught his wife with another man and was heartbroken. He rented an apartment in my area and had started to try to rebuild his life.

One weekend, they started to drink early in the morning. They started out drinking a beer now and then, and as the day progressed they drank more and more. Neighbors said that they were listening to music loudly as they sat on the front porch of the house in which Jim had rented an apartment.

According to Larry, he and Jim had been competitive their entire lives, competing in sports, business, and in high school, seeing who could date the hottest women.

Larry said that Jim was always winning. It had bothered him his whole life that he never could seem to defeat Jim at anything, always being second to Jim's first.

Anyway, the two men were drinking, and sometime in the mid-afternoon they fell back into old habits, one challenging the other to various contests.

It started with arm wrestling; Jim was a lot stronger than Larry, and after several contests that Larry lost, they moved on to Bloody Knuckles.

Bloody Knuckles is a game that every boy knows. You stand facing each other, hands balled into fists, your fists barely touching your opponent's fists. The first one tries to slam his fists down on top of the other's exposed hand before the victim can pull his hands away. If you miss, you lose your turn, and now it's the other guy's turn to smash your knuckles.

It's a contest of speed and concentration. Jim won consistently, and Larry's hands were bruised and swollen from losing the contest so often.

They then moved on to Indian wrestling, and again Jim won. The more they competed, the more that Jim won, and the more they drank.

Larry said it really pissed him off that here he was being a good friend to Jim and supporting him during his divorce, and still Jim was beating him.

Old resentment started to boil up in him, and the day-long drinking fest started to take its toll.

The two men ended up in a fistfight in the front yard of the house.

According to neighbors, they fought for some time, wrestling, punching, sometimes laughing, and sometimes cursing at each other.

They fought sloppily for some time, too drunk to really cause any real damage, and too drunk to stop. Finally, they started to get angry.

After taking some really solid punches to the face, Larry got in a lucky hook and knocked Jim to the ground. Larry was on top of Jim in a second, pummeling his head with blow after blow, the entire day's frustration finally being vented on his best friend's head.

Larry wasn't done when Jim was knocked unconscious from the repeated blows to the head; he climbed off Jim and picked up a large rock from a nearby garden.

He then carried the rock over to where Jim was lying unconscious and slammed it repeatedly into his head, crushing his skull.

We received the call when neighbors heard the cries of anguish from Larry.

They didn't call the cops in this area unless it was really bad, so we knew going in that this would be a bad call.

I arrived and found Larry in the front yard, crying and rocking back and forth. He was holding his best friend's bruised, battered body like a man holds a baby, with Jim's crushed and bloody skull oozing brain matter and blood down the front of Larry's shirt.

Larry told us the story about the day's events, and neighbors filled in the rest. They said that after Larry had finally defeated Jim by crushing his head, he yelled out a defiant primal scream, arms up in the air.

He'd finally defeated the amazing Jim Hayes – finally, after years of trying to defeat him, he had won!

Larry said that he held out his hand to Jim and tried to help him get up, repeatedly asking Jim to get up and acknowledge his victory.

Reality eventually set in, and he realized he'd killed his best friend, beating him to death in an alcohol-fueled rage.

It was a very sad scene.

I interviewed Larry and arrested him.

The case then went to court, and Larry pled guilty; both men's lives were destroyed that night. Central city moved on unaffected by the scene...just another horrible story among many.

21 This Is 911—What Is The Nature Of Your Emergency?

911 WAS INVENTED TO ENABLE anyone in an emergency to call the cops, fire department, or paramedics and get help immediately.

The state laws required our response to 911 calls. No matter what the call, we had to go; however, some people's idea of what constitutes an emergency is a lot different than what the people who invented 911 had in mind.

Here are a couple examples: Penny Steele lived in an apartment in the inner city. She was living with a man, and they both drank heavily. They fought bitter, brutal fights, and she would frequently call us to help her dig herself out of the latest mess she'd buried herself in.

She and her man were totally different people when they were sober; they were both nice, polite, pleasant, and easy going—mellow, even—when they weren't drunk. They were the stereotypical assholes when you added alcohol.

When I got the call to go to their apartment, it was always the scene of a brutal battle if they'd been drinking. I frequently took them both to jail kicking, screaming, spitting, and spewing venomous hatred at me all the way to jail.

One night, the dispatchers called me on the radio and asked me to call them on the phone. This was frequently done when the call required more information than could be put out on the radio.

The dispatcher told me that they had another call at Penny's apartment. They said she'd called in on 911 and asked for the cops to "come quick, her apartment was covered in two inches of water."

The dispatcher said they confirmed over and over that she wanted us to come because her apartment had flooded. This made no sense. She was a frequent flyer, and they knew I knew her as well.

The dispatcher was sure that it was some type of code.

She said that she was afraid that Penny had really got into trouble this time and had to be pretending to call a plumber and complaining about the apartment being flooded because her old man was going to kill her; she was sure that Penny was really in trouble this time.

I agreed that that was the likely reason for the call and started to gear up for the battle about to occur.

The dispatcher said, "We have no back for you; it's too busy—but she's called twice. What do you think, Slick?"

I told her yes, I would go.

I'd fought her old man many times, and if it was too hairy, I could always back out and wait for a back. I'd be careful and keep them apprised of what was happening.

I showed up at the apartment and stood outside for a few minutes, listening. It was creepy silent. Not a sound from the volatile people inside.

I knocked and stepped back away from the door two or three steps.

I heard someone walk to the door, and a kindly female voice said, "Who is it?"

This was the voice she used when she wasn't an angry, psychotic drunk.

I said, "It's the police. Did you call?"

The door opened slowly. I'd already drawn my gun, expecting the worst, ready to shoot whoever came through the door at me; instead, Penny peeked out and smiled when saw me.

"Hi, Slick," she said.

I said, "Hi, Penny. Are you OK?"

She said, "Yes, Come in; I need your help."

Really on edge now, I slowly walked in, gun in both hands, expecting Penny's old man to attack me at any moment.

I said, "Where's your old man?"

She said, "Oh we broke up after that last fight, he left."

That was unbelievable to me.

As I continued to search for him, she said, "Really, he's gone!"

I looked at her and thought, *Oh my God, she's finally killed him.*

I searched the apartment over and over, looking for him dead or alive.

Finally, she sat down, angry. She said, "Why don't you believe me, Slick?"

I told her I'd dealt with them many times, and it had never been easy; this was by far the most reasonable she'd ever been—and she had called 911 about her apartment being flooded. I told her the dispatcher was sure she was in serious trouble this time.

Penny giggled, then said, "I'm sorry, but I had no choice. Come in here."

Still expecting trouble and expecting the worst, I followed (gun still at the ready; our battles had been that intense).

She took me into her bathroom and showed me that her toilet tank had broken and cracked and that water had flooded the bathroom, bedroom, and living room. That was her problem.

I looked around and saw nothing else wrong.

She said, "I didn't know what to do, so I called."

I had her step out of the room; I didn't trust her to be at my back while I was turning off the toilet.

I turned the valve at the base of the toilet off, then brought her back in and told her how to shut it off in the future.

She was so relieved, she grabbed me and gave me a big hug.

I was surprised, and I admit not really being sure what to think. She was so fast, I was sure I'd get stabbed or bitten or something; I wasn't expecting to be hugged.

I left the apartment and phoned dispatch, telling them it really was about the apartment flooding. I ended the account with Penny hugging me.

The dispatcher said, "You're shitting me?"

"Nope, not this time."

Another 911 call.

Dispatch said over the radio that some guy had called and that he sounded really high. They suspected that he was hallucinating because he was making no sense. He called 911 to report some problem with his furnace, saying that he could hear a bird inside it. They said he was very rude and that they were sure he was a tweeker.

I arrived at the house with another cop as back up.

We contacted the guy who called, and at the time he seemed OK; not high, not crazy. He asked us to come in, and we did go inside the home.

I asked him why he'd called.

He said, "Where are your tools?"

Not the usual response I'd get to that question, so I asked again, "Why did you call?"

He rolled his eyes and said, "Jesus Christ! I told them to tell you to bring tools!"

I decided to play along; I didn't know what his issues were, but he obviously had something going on.

I said, "Well, first, before I get the tools, I need to know the problem, sir."

He said, "Oh! OK, follow me."

He walked to the basement doorway and went down the stairs ahead of us.

We followed carefully, a little on edge.

When we got to the basement, he put one hand on his hip and pointed with the other at the old furnace in the basement.

I said, "So, what's wrong with it?"

He rolled his eyes again, sighed, and said, "Don't you people communicate with each other? No wonder crime is so out of hand in this city! Imbeciles!"

I said, "Sir, maybe you can explain the problem?"

He sighed again and said, "I have a bird in my furnace, officer, and I want you to get it out."

I said, "What?"

He said slowly, in a very condescending voice, "I said I have a goddamn bird in my furnace, and I want it out—now!"

I stepped closer to the furnace, and sure enough, I could hear a bird trapped in the flue, chirping and scratching.

Apparently, it had somehow fallen down the chimney into the furnace.

I turned to my backup, smiled, and said, "There is a bird!"

My back up laughed and said, "Really?"

The guy was livid.

He yelled, "So what are you gonna do about it? Isn't this what you're supposed to do? I call you, and you come and fix the problem? Fix the problem, geniuses!"

I'd had enough of this arrogant prick's shit.

He wasn't crazy; he was simply an arrogant dickhead.

I said, "We'll fix nothing—and you better change your fuckin' tone real quick. You called 911 to report a bird in your furnace; that's abuse of the 911 system, asswipe. Keep it up with your attitude, and I'll take your ass to jail."

I continued, "We have our tools with us at all times: a gun, tazer, pepper spray, and ASP. We're not here to fix your goddamn furnace— we're here to save your ass from a burglar, murderer, the crazed tweeker, or the neighbor who's sick of your shitty attitude and wants to beat the fuck out of you! You call the HVAC repair guy for your furnace and the bird inside of it; you don't call us."

He suddenly had an epiphany—the five-watt bulb burning brightly inside of his head—and decided to walk us politely back to the door and wish us a good day.

22 Fate Can Be An Evil Bitch

SEVERAL WEEKS HAD GONE BY, and the college ride along had never returned.

I was pretty sure I'd scared her off and that there was no way she'd come back. I'd forgotten all about the business suit and jacketed woman trying to fit in on my calls in the inner city while everyone stared at her.

One day I came out of briefing, and the dispatcher said I had a visitor at the front desk. I never had visitors; I frequently had complaints, but never a visitor.

I thought to myself, *What now?*

Maybe the wife was serving me divorce papers. We hadn't gotten along for years. Could I be that lucky?

Anyway, I went to the desk expecting the worst, and guess who showed up? The college ride-along.

She'd remembered that she couldn't come dressed as Executive Of The Year and had showed up in blue jeans and a sweatshirt, wearing a jacket and ball cap. The transformation was amazing.

She said, "Remember me?"

Stunned, I said, "Um, ya. So where you been?"

She'd been in a car crash and had totaled her car, and this was the first chance she had to finish the course and complete the ride-along to get credit for school.

She laughed and said, "Is this plain enough?"

I guess it was plain enough.

Now I realized why everyone was staring at her; it wasn't the business suit she'd worn before.

We started out as usual, only this time the tables were turned.

She got in the car and said, "So...no comments, no talking, don't touch the radio or the heater, and stay by you at all times, right?"

She was smiling this playful, mischievous smile.

I said, "Ya, right" thinking to myself, *Shit, I am in real trouble now; this woman was hot as hell and was not in the least bit intimidated.*

It was payback time for me being such a prick.

She hadn't left intimidated; she had left plotting and, scheming, ready to return and issue some payback.

We handled a couple of calls, and then went to get a drink. Instead this time she got out first and walked in ahead of me. I am sure she did it to make sure I watched her walk in.

I admit, the tactic worked. I was speechless. Wondering how the hell I had missed the fact that she was hot as hell.

I got a drink and waited while she took her time. The clerk was the same guy from before, and he whispered as I checked out, "What the hell is it with you and the supermodels?"

I said, "No shit! Can you believe that is the same girl from a few weeks ago?"

He said, "No shit? Really? Wow!"

"Ya," I replied, "It is gonna be a long night."

I was right—but not in the way I thought it would be.

We left and started to patrol the inner city.

Slowly, we started to talk about her car crash and what had been happening since we last met.

It was pretty uncomfortable being in the car with her. The tables had definitely turned on me, and I was hoping for calls to keep my mind occupied.

Every call that we went on, the people continued to stare and whisper to each other while they watched her.

Women would be instantly defensive and scowl at her, looking down their noses at her.

The men would be sidetracked and distracted and have a hard time paying attention while I questioned them, wanting to turn and see where she was or stare at her.

The transformation was amazing to me; how just one thing, a person's appearance, could totally change the dynamics of how difficult it was to handle a call effectively.

The reality was she was that strikingly beautiful. Finally, a call came in where even she couldn't distract the bystanders.

Car crashes are among my least favorite calls.

Cops are like hunters in my mind, and there are trackers and trappers.

Trackers like to pursue the bad guy, learning the street, reading signs of the jungle that's the inner city, watching the gang signs, graffiti, learning the hangouts and back routes that drug dealers worked. It was a mental game of chess, and to me, much more of a challenge. I loved it.

Traffic cops are more like trappers. They set a trap and wait to see who falls into it. Anyone who speeds is caught; doesn't matter if it's grandpa and grandma on a drive—they speed, they get a ticket.

To a traffic cop, they're called "Violators"; they violated the law.

To me, that was mindless work. I couldn't stand it. I hated it and talked shit to traffic cops every chance I got.

We got a call of a traffic accident at 59th and Reynolds.

I groaned. First, I had to deal with the Playmate Of The Year riding with me all night; now I had a car crash that would take hours of paperwork and keep me from being available to handle the "real calls" that were so frequent in my area.

We headed towards 59th Street as the information on the crash continued to come in.

Rosa Sosa, Anita Delgado, and Tira Santillian were driving around the city, cruising the streets, talking to friends, and checking out guys as they drove the city streets.

The girls were seventeen, sixteen, and fifteen years old. They would usually have been drinking beer and looking for a party to go to, hoping to meet up with some hot guys from school. Tonight, however, was different.

The three girls were each a couple months pregnant, and instead of beer they were drinking chocolate milk.

They were sharing the plans they had for their children's future, talking about possible names if the child were a boy or a girl. They were each excited and happy and sharing their thoughts with each other about the future.

Lloyd Sears, Brent Rowe, and James Nye were out that night as well. They were at a party, drinking beers and hanging out, trying to pick up some women in one of the inner city apartment complexes.

A fight had broken out, and shots had been fired. They were SP-13 gang members, and another family from SP-13 had shown up at the party. The two families hated each other, and a battle broke out.

The three guys jumped into a car and thought they were being pursued by their rivals. Lloyd was driving and had no intention of being shot. He hit the gas and wouldn't let up.

He was crossing the city, trying to lose the pursing shooters. He felt that he had to make it more dangerous for the shooters to chase him so they'd stop shooting. He started to run stop signs, gaining speed as he crossed the city.

Rowe would tell me later that they were yelling at him to stop. The shooters had dropped off and they were safe, but Sears wouldn't let up. He continued crossing intersection after intersection, gaining speed as he went. No matter what Rowe and Nye said, he wouldn't let off the gas and wouldn't stop as they blasted through stop sign after stop sign.

He made it through five intersections untouched and had reached sixty miles per hour when they approached 59th and Reynolds.

Rosa, Anita, and Tira had just left a small convenience store.

They'd stopped to use the rest room, laughing about how much more they had to pee since they became pregnant. Then, all three of them got into the front seat of Rosa's car.

Rosa was driving, Anita was sitting in the middle, and Tira was on the far right nearest the door.

They decided to go west on 59th and hit the main drag. They were looking for some cute guys they saw earlier and wanted to flirt with them, see if they could get them to pull over and talk. They had six blocks to go to reach the main boulevard.

When they reached Reynolds, they were all laughing about a joke that Rosa had made about her boyfriend.

Suddenly, Tira saw a bright flash of light as they crossed Reynolds and tried to scream.

I arrived at the intersection a few moments after the call of a crash came in, and I wasn't prepared for what it would look like. I stopped, stunned for a moment, trying to figure it out.

Rosa's car had been T-boned, hit on the passenger side at sixty miles per hour as Lloyd entered the intersection; he'd ignored the stop sign and slammed into the car full of pregnant young girls.

Tira caught a brief glimpse of his headlights before he slammed into the car door inches away from her.

The momentum of the impact drove Rosa's car sideways across the intersection, off of the road, and across the front yard of the house on the opposite side of the street from where Lloyd had entered the intersection. The car slid sideways across the front yard until it hit a tree. All three girls were inside.

Lloyd's car continued to coast forward. After losing all of its momentum from slamming into the girls' car, it came to rest on the side of the road in front of the same house that Rosa's car had slid across. Both cars were destroyed.

Lloyd Sears and Nye were somehow uninjured in the impact, and each ran from the scene. Rowe said his legs felt funny, and he couldn't run. He later admitted he was too stunned to think clearly and couldn't have run if he tried.

When I arrived, Rosa was still behind the wheel, conscious and awake. Anita was unconscious, hanging backwards over the front seat. Her torso was in the back seat of the car and her legs were in the front seat. Her pelvis was shattered. Tira was dead, hanging out the shattered passenger window, basically half in the car and half out.

I checked her pulse; it was gone. I checked her eyes; her pupils were blown, and all brain activity was gone. She died from the impact, and her unborn child had died with her. The other two girls were still alive, and I advised medical of the situation, requesting they hurry.

Once the supervisors arrived, they gave the call to the traffic units and called in the traffic accident reconstruction specialists. They determined that the speed Lloyd was traveling was sixty mph. when he hit the three girls. There were no skids; he hadn't tried to stop at all.

The remaining two girls were carefully removed from the crash by paramedics. Tira was also removed and transported to the hospital so her family could identify her body. I was tasked with locating witnesses—and with this being the inner city, few people would cooperate.

My ride-along watched all this and actually became a huge help. She noticed Rowe struggling to stand. He was hiding in the crowd that had gathered, and she went to talk to him. He admitted to her that he'd been in the car.

She came to me and said, "That guy was in the car," pointing at Rowe. I rolled my eyes; I didn't believe her.

Every ride-along that ever rode with me thought they were special and could see what we didn't. The last thing I needed was her photogenic ass feeling that she could make a difference or save the day.

She grabbed my arm and said, "Listen to me! He was in the car; he can barely stand up because he's hurt."

I looked at her and saw that she meant it. This was not some narcissistic need to be noticed; she really was trying to help.

I went over and spoke to Rowe, and he told me that he was in the car. He told me what happened then asked me to help him. He couldn't feel his legs; he could stand, but he had no feeling at all in his legs. I called medical to him immediately and got him transported to the hospital.

This was a fatal hit and run, and the ride-along had found the only one of the occupants of the car hidden in the crowd. After this call, I looked at my college ride-along in a new light, and I listened to her comments as we rode together.

I continued to investigate and helped the traffic guys do their thing. Detectives were also brought in on the case and started to look for Lloyd and Nye.

Lloyd was caught later that morning and gave a full written confession. He was convicted of automobile homicide and sentenced to prison.

Rowe would be a key witness as to what had happened inside the car before the accident. His spine was damaged, and he would have medical problems for the rest of his life.

Rosa and Anita both survived the crash; however, both of them lost their unborn children from the violence of the impact.

I went home that morning and was pretty shook up. I couldn't get the image of the Tira hanging out of the car out of my mind.

My wife at the time asked me what was wrong, and I told her the story, hopeful that maybe she'd be able to understand just once what I went through. She sighed and said, "That's so sad that those girls were pregnant and not married."

I looked at her in disbelief. I said, "What? What do you mean?"

She replied, "It's just sad that they had no morals and were pregnant and not married."

I wondered silently, *Who and what the fuck are you?*

I never told anyone, but I didn't sleep for three days after the crash; it really hit me hard. The girl hanging out of the car dead, all three girls' babies dead. None of them had done anything to deserve what happened to them.

This was another thing I hated about traffic: the victims were random. There was no logic to any of it. I could make no sense of it.

I did, however, listen to the hot college ride-along from that point on. She had earned my trust.

23 Cops Are Paranoid For A Reason

PEOPLE ARE ALWAYS TALKING SHIT about how cops are paranoid.

They go to the mall and see bad guys everywhere. They go out for a drive and constantly worry about someone running the stop signs and hitting them. Don't even think about going out to eat in uniform unless you know the chef and the waiter. (Unless, of course, you're the Chief at one of the city's elite restaurants; no need to worry there, right?).

"Daywalkers" think that there's no way anything could happen. The rules are there to protect them, and of course everyone follows the rules...Ya, right.

Cops are funny about what they eat for a reason. The very nature of our job entitles us to information the rest of the world will never know – and sometimes it's stuff we *really* don't want to know.

There was this very popular restaurant on the east side of the city. It had a 50s décor and had food and soft drinks from the era. It did a lot of business. Older people in the city would fill the place, feeling it reminded them of a simpler, safer time.

The restaurant had music from the 50s, and the walls were plastered with posters from the 50s and pictures of movies and musicians from the era. Basically, it was a place to relive the memories of times gone by. The city's day people loved it.

One night, we got a call to the west side. It was called in as a domestic dispute. When we got the call, the woman who called was hysterical and in a rage. She was angry and sounded really upset. The patrol arrived and started to try and sort out what was going on. It was quite a mess.

The husband wouldn't talk to the cops, and there was no evidence that there had been a fight. The officers split the couple apart and tried to find out what had happened.

This was common procedure for most domestics. It allowed the couple to talk frankly about what the problem was and maybe open up a bit more than they would in the same room with each other.

The cop with the woman heard this story: they owned a large male German Shepherd, and it faithfully followed the husband wherever he went. It was a very loyal dog. It was the wife's dog, however, and this had irritated her immensely.

She did everything she could to try to win the dog's favor: bacon treats, long walks, and baby talk telling him what a great dog he was. Nothing worked.

As soon as the man walked in, the dog's ears would perk up, its tail would wag, and it would bark excitedly. As far as the dog was concerned, the woman had dropped off the face of the earth.

She was really mad explaining this to the officer, so mad she threw up a couple times, literally retching, and puking as she told the story.

The officer said that he thought she was crazy for being so angry about the dog liking her husband that it made her sick.

She continued. Tonight, she'd been at work at a local auto parts manufacturing company. Normally, she got off work at a specific hour. It was the same time every night; her schedule was written in stone. It never waivered. It never changed.

Tonight, however, the parts had been built, and the contract had been fulfilled ahead of schedule.

So, the manager had let the workers go early for the first time in years. Normally, they had to stay late to make the quota, but not tonight.

The wife was really excited to come home early.

Getting the unexpected time off made her really happy; she'd be able to come home and spend time with her husband. She emphasized this point to the cop, saying, "Imagine that I was excited to come home and see that motherfucker!"

The cop already knew what had happened. It happened a lot with our job.

One spouse or the other would get some unexpected time off and come home to find their better half locked in a passionate oral embrace with the neighbor's genitals—or even worse, the best friend of the unsuspecting spouse.

The rage and disgust suddenly made sense to the officer. That was what the cop thought as he listened to the story unfold.

He started to add his two cents about how he understood what she was feeling and asked if there was any way she could stay at a friend's house for the evening.

She was having none of this patronizing shit.

She pointed her finger at the cop and said, "Look, fucker, you have no idea what I feel! None! Shut the fuck up!"

The cop was new and didn't know yet never to assume anything on the street; never.

She chewed his ass for a while until he said, "OK, OK. Let me guess: you caught him with another woman, and you're pissed off. I'm sorry, lady, but it happens all the time."

The woman laughed and threw up her arms.

She said, "Really? You're telling me this happens all the time?"

He said, "Yes, spouses frequently come home unexpectedly and find their husband or wife having sex with another person."

It was heartbreaking, and he understood her pain, he said later as he told me this story.

She stared at him for a moment, then laughed hard and loud. A weird, angry, heartbroken laugh.

She shook her head violently and gagged again, coughing and spitting out bile.

She quietly said, "If only that was it."

She was silent for a moment, and the cop took that to mean that she'd caught her husband with another man.

It happened. Not as frequently, but it happened. He explained that he'd seen that as well.

He considered himself a veteran of the department now.

He'd been on the department five years and thought he'd seen it all. Well, he was almost right.

She looked at him with a dark, knowing look.

She was about to blow his mind, and she knew it.

She'd share her shock and disgust and put the young cop in his place.

She stood up and crossed her arms, gathering herself. He said she stared right into his eyes and started to tell him the rest of the story.

She had arrived home early and saw that her husband was home as well. He was a chef at the 50s-themed diner I told you about earlier.

They had both gotten off early that night, and neither knew the other was getting off outside their normal schedule. She was really excited that they both had time off together; unexpected time off.

She quietly sneaked into the house.

Dropping off her purse and keys quietly on the couch, she then slowly took off her clothes, leaving on her shoes and socks as she playfully stripped, quietly sneaking through the house, looking for her man.

When she stopped outside the bedroom, she'd dropped nearly all of her clothing. She was nervous with anticipation, hoping the expected encounter would be all that she'd built it up to be in her mind.

She said she dropped her panties at the bedroom door, then opened the door, expecting to surprise her husband; instead, she found this.

The husband had been working at the "diner" that evening, like she said. It was his normal shift. The restaurant had been slow that night for some reason. That was the nature of the fast food business. It's feast or famine. You're either so slow that you can't pay the light bill or so stacked up with customers waiting to get in that you can't possibly seat them all.

His manager had let him go early. The manager couldn't justify keeping two chefs in the kitchen with no customers, and it was his turn to be called off. He left the restaurant two full hours early. He arrived home to the excited, barking German shepherd—his best buddy! He let the dog out and started to read the paper.

A few minutes passed, and the dog was back at the door, scratching, wanting to be let in. He got up and let the dog in, then went back to take a shower. He was still kind of dirty from working over the grill at the diner and wanted to clean up.

Normally, this would lead up to a "Trojan" moment or maybe one of those funny lubricant commercials with rockets going off and the couple afterwards lying exhausted in bed; the showered husband and naked wife surprising each other, each coming home early and not telling the other.

Instead, the wife opened the door and found her freshly showered, soap-smelling husband lying on top of her German Shepherd.

He was sucking the dog's definitely erect penis and cupping its testicles while the dog was cooperatively staying very still.

They were all surprised by her sudden appearance in the room.

The cop told me he was sure he had heard her wrong.

But then he realized it all fit, her gagging and puking. The rage and disgust.

He said to me later, "What the fuck do you say to that? The woman caught her husband giving their dog a blowjob! How do you say you understand that?"

He said to make matters worse (in his mind) the wife was really amazingly attractive.

He said he thought to himself, *What the fuck, dude? You got a beautiful wife—and you wanna blow the German Shepherd?*

The wife glared at the cop and said, "What do you have to say to that, officer?! Still wanna tell me how you can understand my disgust? Well?"

She said, "Now, the dog makes perfect fucking sense as well! No fucking wonder the dog never liked me."

The cop said he was silent. He had no reply. He said he started to feel sick himself.

They arrested the husband for bestiality. He didn't deny the wife's claims and told the "veteran" cop he'd had a "problem" for years.

The beautiful wife started gagging again at this revelation and ran for the bathroom, dry heaving as the cops removed her husband from the house.

They put him into a patrol car to be booked into jail later.

So when you think of cops as paranoid and you're talking trash, wondering why they only go to certain restaurants, you may want to pay attention.

They may know who prepares the food.

24 Recognizing Who It Is Matters

ONE NIGHT, I HEARD A call go out in my area. I was busy writing reports, and the only reason I took notice was that the call came in as a loud party.

The complainant said that a large group of black men were playing music really loud and that they refused to turn the music off. The caller wanted the music turned down.

I heard the usual two units get dispatched then I heard Sergeant Peabody call out and say that he was also going to the call.

I knew this would end poorly if he pulled his usual shit. He wasn't known for diplomacy. The other two units assigned were new guys and would do whatever he said to do, even if it was obviously the wrong thing to do.

This was the new, up-and-coming cop's way of working: follow orders, no matter what.

The department had hired followers for years, trying to get rid of those that would think for themselves and not follow blindly.

I arrived to find the front porch of the house occupied by twelve guys listening to loud rap music. They refused to back down to three cops. I made it four.

I watched as Sergeant Peabody tried to bully his way onto the porch. He turned off the music, and then asked who rented the apartment. No one answered him, and as soon as he left the porch, the music went back up. Tempers were flaring.

This was gonna go to shit fast. It was no longer about music being too loud; it was now about respect and power. Who would be the first to blink?

Sergeant Peabody walked to each one of us and whispered that under no circumstances were we backing down; these motherfuckers would learn a lesson today to not disrespect the cops. I listened to him and nodded.

He had such a Black and White way of thinking. There were other alternatives, but he didn't see things that way. He was Black and White in everything he did, and in this case it was quite literally Black vs. White. It was also twelve against four.

I searched the group on the porch, looking for a leader among them.

Finally, I saw who the guy leading the defiant "stand against the man" was. It was a guy I had worked with and against many times on the street and in the Gang Task Force.

His street name was Ebony.

He was a major pain in the ass. He was the kind of guy who would always fight when he had a crowd around him. He never, ever fought one-on-one with anyone. He needed the crowd to feel safe and anonymous.

They had Ebony working them up, and we had Peabody. Two mental midgets not giving a shit about the outcome of the brawl that was definitely about to occur.

I thought about that for a minute and realized I needed to find a way to make the most out of Ebony's need to remain anonymous.

I stepped to the side quietly and switched frequencies on our radio. I had dispatch check Ebony by his real name on warrants. He had a minor warrant for a traffic infraction. I asked them to mark the inquiry into the warrant as 'Information Only Request' and went back to the group.

I called out to Ebony as he stood on the porch, quietly at first, then louder each time until he could no longer ignore me. I asked him to step away from his group and talk to me.

He said, "Fuck ya, motherfucker, I'll talk to you," as he hopped off the porch, jumping over the railing and strutting towards me in an attempt to prove that he wasn't afraid.

Several voices in his group said, "Kick his ass, man," "Don't take that cop's shit", and then, "We got them outnumbered!" "This shit is gonna be fun—kicking the popo's ass!"

We walked to the corner, away from anyone being able to hear what we said.

I said, "Hey, man, you see what's gonna happen here? This is gonna go to shit real quick."

He replied, "That's right, popo, it is! So you better take your white ass back to your car before it gets kicked!"

I laughed (getting pissed off) and said, "Look, man, I know you, and you know me. I was there the night you and Bobby kicked the shit out of Boo Rock. I know who you are, and if you don't know me, then maybe you need to shut the hell up and learn."

He replied, "So who the fuck am I, Mr. White cop?"

He glared at me, challenging me.

I told him his real name, and he stopped, stunned.

I continued, "I checked, and you have an outstanding warrant as well. No one here knows that except me."

He looked at me and quietly said, "I'm listening."

I said, "If this does go to shit, a lot of your homies are gonna get fucked up, no doubt a lot of my homies as well. You may have us outnumbered at the moment, but what you don't know is two K-9 units are on their way. The Land sharks are coming, so I'm giving you a chance to show real leadership."

He nodded and said, "Fo sho, Fo sho. Go on."

"The guy over there, the Sergeant, has already said that no way are we leaving or backing down. He wants to fight—and believe me, if he gets his chance, a lot of your homies will get seriously fucking hurt; that doesn't have to happen."

He was listening now, quietly watching the other cops as they watched us talk.

He said, "What do you suggest, man?"

I said, "Talk to your homies. Tell them I recognized the stripes, and out of respect to you we're letting you all leave. You have a warrant, and if this goes to shit, it'll all come back to you because I'm the only one here who knows the name of anyone in your group …do you get that? You're the only one here I know, you're in charge, and this will be on your head if it goes to shit."

He nodded and thought for a minute. He was no longer anonymous; there would be no hiding from this.

I could see I'd reached him. He agreed and made a big spectacle out of shaking my hand and thanking me.

He then strutted back to the porch and said, "Hey, fellahs, the man has shown me the respect I'm due. He recognized the stripes. Let's go; there's no need to make a stand here." (Whatever the fuck that meant, I don't know, and I don't care; it worked.)

No one wanted to fight, but no one wanted to appear to be afraid as well.

With Ebony willing to take the first step and announce that I'd recognized his "stripes", they could leave and save face with each other.

They did leave—and fast.

They really didn't want to fight, and neither did most of us – everyone, that is, except Sergeant Peabody. He was furious with me. He called me a fucking coward and stormed off.

Another night and another loud party.

We were called this time to a loud party in the 4200 block of Field. The landlord had rented the apartment to several known 18th street gang members, and they had invited the majority of the set to the apartment for a party.

I was called by one of the units there. They thought because I'd just left Gangs that I may have a rapport with the gang members and get them to shut down the party without a fight.

I tried to explain that 18th street hadn't been friendly with me and that West Side 18th street had actually had a hit out on me.

They laughed. "Ya, Ya, no one puts hits out on cops, Slick! You're so damn paranoid! You watch way too much TV. You're like 'Spooky Mulder' on the X files always seeing conspiracies!"

I sighed and said, "OK! If you say so."

I walked up to the door, knowing this wouldn't end well.

They'd already knocked once and asked the party to break up, and the person that they talked to agreed to break up the party and closed the door. Fifteen minutes later, nothing had happened.

I knocked, and the door opened. I recognized the guy who answered as Penguin from South Side 18th street. I told him the party was over; it was time to go.

He did the same thing as before, agreed to leave, and tried to close the door in my face.

I stuck my foot in the door so it wouldn't shut.

I said, "Look, motherfucker, we're trying to be nice—but if you push the issue, we'll break up the party by force. We'll put every fucking one of you in jail. You make the choice."

Penguin backed into the apartment and yelled out, "Pacman is here and wants to break up the party. He says we're all bitches and we will go without a fight!"

Shit…that wasn't what I had hoped for, but it was what I expected. I was never considered an ally to 18th street.

We ended up calling every available unit in the city to the party to make a statement to the gang.

When the cops show up and ask you politely to leave, take the easy way out and leave.

We took as many as we could to jail, and the others took off quickly; wisely escaping into the night.

There were some that fought us initially, but after the rest saw the outcome of those fights, they gave up. It all came down to respect.

Never try to close the door in the popo's face when you're getting a break.

25 Bright Eyes

ONE NIGHT, I WAS SITTING on one of the main boulevards, talking with another cop.

It was snowing hard, and it was cold. We all got off the roads in weather like that, hoping not to have to drive too much.

As we talked, I noticed a woman walking down the road in nothing but a thin sleeping shirt and slippers. I said, "Hey, man, look at this: what's wrong with this picture?"

We watched while she walked down the sidewalk, aimlessly stopping and looking around, then walking again. She looked lost, and if she had been older I would have suspected that she was an escapee from a convalescent center, maybe someone who had Alzheimer's and thought they were on a beach somewhere in the Bahamas.

We crossed the street and stopped her, asking her name and what she was doing. She tried to give a response, but it made no sense.

We asked the same thing over and over and got gibberish as a response. We could tell that she thought that what she said made sense; watching her eyes and body language, it was obvious she knew we were there, but we couldn't make any sense of what she said.

We talked it over, and for her protection we decided to take her to the Emergency Room and see if we could commit her to the psych ward. We had no idea who she was or where she belonged.

While the other cop was taking her to the hospital, I tried to back-track her footprints in the snow. It was snowing really hard, and I lost her tracks.

After five blocks, I knew about where she had been, but she'd wandered back and forth, walking in circles and sometimes doubling back. It was apparent she'd been out walking in the cold and snow for some time.

By the time I arrived at the Emergency Room about a half an hour later, the nurses had discovered her name; from that, they pulled up an address in their databases. They said she was diagnosed as a schizo-phrenic and that she had a daughter, a small infant.

We all looked at each other, worried about what that could mean. As lost as she was, and unaware of her surroundings, who knows where the baby was or in what condition?

I asked them for the last known address they had for her and cross-referenced it with the police department's database. We had two addresses that were different from their database.

I checked all three.

The first two were old addresses, and the people weren't happy to have been awakened at 3 a.m. looking for the ex-tenants. The third was a small garage in the rear of a house. The owners had renovated the garage and made it into a very small home.

I knocked on the door, and it swung open.

I was in central city, so I assumed nothing.

I pulled my gun out, ready to scrap with whatever came my way.

I called out, "Police! Is anyone here?"

I looked around the small house and immediately was creeped out.

The woman definitely lived here; the place was creepy as hell.

She had cut pictures out of every baby magazine that she could find, specifically the eyes of the infants. Then she plastered the infants' eyes all over the apartment.

Every square inch was a pair of baby eyes staring back at you. Every wall, every flat surface, every window covered with baby eyes glued to the surface. There were no pictures of complete babies; just the eyes. The shit creeped me out big time!

I was now even more apprehensive about the welfare of the child.

Searching the home, I found a crib and diapers, some baby clothes as well, but no baby.

I came into the kitchen and noticed that the oven was on and that there was smoke coming out of the oven.

I thought, *Oh shit! The crazy bitch has cooked her baby.*

I rushed to the oven and opened it.

There was a hunk of meat in the oven that was about the size of an infant. I could see what looked like legs and arms as well. I thought, *Fuck, I hate this job.*

Smoke came rolling out of the oven into the house, and the smoke alarms finally kicked in.

I looked for a potholder to try and get the pan with the smoking baby out of the oven.

Finally, I found one and removed the pan.

I was sick to my stomach with all the babies' eyes on the walls watching everything I did.

Trying to keep it together mentally, I waited for the smoke to clear and prepared to call for CSI.

Finally, I could see the baby, and the relief was incredible. What I thought was a baby baking in the oven was actually a large chicken.

I said a quiet, "Fuck me! This shit sucks ass!"

I threw the smoking chicken outside and cleared the smoke from the house.

I seriously thought that she had baked her child, and when I saw the shape of the chicken with four appendages, my mind filled in the rest.

I had to take a minute before I went back to the Emergency Room. This shit was traumatic; even though the child had not been baked, in my mind for a moment it had been.

I went back to the Emergency Room and told the other officer about the house, the baby eyes, and the oven.

We both laughed. It was all we could do.

By that time, we'd both seen a lot on the street; we knew anything was possible.

Still, we didn't know where the child was.

The Emergency Room had another point of contact that was in another state, and we called it.

The child was there. They had taken the child from the woman because she had gone off her medication and they didn't feel that the child would be safe with her. We all breathed a sigh of relief.

Several weeks afterwards, I'd have nightmares about the baby eyes and the burnt chicken in the oven. I'd wake up covered in sweat, breathing hard, thinking, *WOW! Man, that call really got to me.*

Sometimes, it wasn't the life-threatening calls that messed you up mentally.

Sometimes, it was simple shit like baby eyes quietly staring at you from all over the walls and ceiling and a burned chicken in the oven.

26 Bring Your Milking Boots

EVERY ONCE IN A WHILE, I'd bump into one of the guys from my old department.

I left because I felt opportunities would be better in the city, and I felt like I'd never fit in there. The old department was rural law enforcement, and I had no feel for it at all.

I grew up in the city and had no idea what the difference was between a Western saddle and an English saddle. I didn't know the different breeds of cattle, chickens, or horses. I was lost in the world of rural law enforcement.

I could recognize the difference between a West Side 18th street gang member from a SP-13 gang member just from the way they dressed and how they carried themselves; still, I tried to understand the guys I worked with at that department and occasionally went to get a drink with them during slow times at work.

This incident would forever seal the fact that I didn't belong in that world.

There was a new convenience store on the border of the city and the county and both departments would mingle there during breaks.

I came in one night just to see who was there and what was new.

I saw two of the guys I used to work with when I walked in. They were sitting in a corner and called me over.

I bought a drink and headed over as they broke into a hearty laugh. I asked what was so funny. They wouldn't comment, instead asking what the latest was at the city.

We talked about the politics of the city police work, and the reality was that it was nothing compared to the politics in the sheriff's department.

We all knew that was a meat grinder that could destroy your career in a second.

Eventually, we ran out of things to talk about, and I said, "So what were you guys laughing about when I came up?"

They looked at each other quietly for a minute, and finally one of them started to talk.

He said, "You know how I own a dairy?"

I said I did.

He went on to tell me again how his family had owned the dairy for some time, and now he was running the family business.

He was about forty at the time and had recently been promoted to Sergeant.

He had been pretty successful since the new Sheriff had been elected and had risen through the ranks pretty quickly.

He said that he'd been forced to hire a lot of workers to keep up with the demands of the dairy and had resorted to hiring illegal aliens.

He said that he'd had a few problems with the workers and had to straighten one of them out.

He said, "I sort of wanted to make an example of him, ya know?"

I could see the gleam in his eyes, and I thought to myself, *That's what you get for asking, dumbass!*

He continued and told me that he and a couple of the large farm hands had discussed what to do to make an example of the outspoken illegal farm hand. They'd come up with a plan and waited for him to speak up before they implemented it.

They said that they didn't have to wait long. The worker started talking shit, and they grabbed him.

I thought they were gonna kick the shit out of him—but WOW, was I wrong.

He said that they brought him to a post and tied him to it, arms behind his back. They then brought up a young calf.

At this point, the other guy bursts out laughing; it was one of those good ol' boy laughs I never got used to.

The Sergeant said that he held the calf while the other two dropped his pants.

They were both laughing now.

He said he walked the calf up to the shit-talking guy's dick, and immediately the calf rammed the guy in the nuts. Then it started sucking on his dick.

Calves butt their heads into the cows' udders several times—hard—to get the milk to drop; this is normal behavior for a calf.

The calf kept butting the guy in the groin, then sucking on his dick.

They let the calf slam into the guy over and over for about ten minutes until he passed out from the pain.

This was the funny story they were telling each other when I walked in.

The Sergeant said that they never had any problem with any of the other workers after that and that the guy never came back to work after he left that day.

I looked at both of them and remembered that feeling I used to get when I worked with them, the feeling that the entire world had gone to shit.

The crime in the city, I understood; this good ol' boy shit was beyond me.

I got up and said, "Well, you two have fun sodomizing your cattle and chickens. I'm gonna go back to the streets; at least there I know no one would think of some fucked up shit like that!"

They didn't find the sodomizing comment funny at all; must have struck a nerve, I guess. Who knows? I don't wanna know.

27 Always Wear Your Helmet

SOMETIMES, YOU GO ON A call that's nothing close to what you think it'll be; nothing that you have any frame of reference for or would even know existed.

I had one of those calls one night.

I was dispatched to a home in central city. It was a large house and was home to a very large family. Grandparents, parents, an aunt and uncle, and kids all living in the same home. There was still plenty of room. The home was that big. Just one of the old mansions that had been built around the turn of the century by a wealthy railroad tycoon and was now in the worst part of town.

The call was supposed to be an unattended death, meaning someone had died and the family had called to request a mortician.

We always went to ensure that there was no foul play, nothing suspicious about the death.

I arrived at the same time as my back up, and we went to the door of the home. A middle-aged woman came to the door, crying, and asked us to come in. Everyone in the house was crying and upset. The mood was very sad.

There was also a weird undercurrent of relief. It wasn't the normal "unattended death" feeling from the family.

You always have to be paying attention to the things that are not being said in the communication when you're on a call. That's where the real details and information are.

I was already on alert. This wasn't the norm. There were tears, but the emotions were mixed…. grief and an overwhelming sense that this family was relieved that death had finally came.

We stopped for a moment and observed one family member after another showing the same conflicted emotions. I commented on this to the woman.

I said, "It appears that your family is in grief and relief at the same time," making a statement, not a question, waiting to see where the comment took her. She nodded in agreement and asked us to follow her to the basement of the home. We walked down a very old staircase to a renovated basement.

By this time, we had both unsnapped our holsters, and our hands were resting on the handgrips of the guns.

You never knew who you could trust or what you were being drawn into; this was really weird. So, you always assumed the worst and prepared.

We arrived at the basement, and nothing happened.

The woman began to explain to us that they had done all they could to protect the "girl."

They'd slept in shifts, each of the adult members taking turns at keeping watch. She said that they'd only let the "watch" slip for a moment. They thought she was safe, then realized no one was watching her.

I said, "So where is she?"

She opened a door to a room off a hallway, and there was a female lying naked, face up on the floor.

She had a large claw hammer on one hand, and her head was severely beaten. Her right eye was swollen shut, and the cheekbone on the opposite side of the swollen eye was caved in. She had several large dents in her skull.

The hammer was covered in blood, and hair and the blood still appeared to be moist. She appeared to be about twelve years old.

I looked around the room and saw blood splatters on the wall, typical of a homicide scene where a person had been beaten to death. There was a motorcycle helmet in the corner that was very pitted and damaged. It had blood on it as well. The whole scene was typical of a murder scene.

I looked at my back up, and we exchanged a look that communicated with eye contact only that this was not what it appeared to be. This couldn't have been an unattended death; it appeared to be a homicide.

I asked the woman how this had happened.

She said the girl was born "different" and that they'd tried to take care of her.

I asked the girl's age, and she said the girl was thirty-five. That wasn't possible; this girl looked twelve.

She said that the girl was born with a mental illness that caused her to try to harm herself. They had kept watch over her since the illness was discovered when she was very young. The woman said that the family kept her locked into the motorcycle helmet; she had to wear it night and day, or she'd slam her head into the wall or hit herself with a hard object like a hammer until she was stopped by someone else or knocked herself out. The girl had nearly killed herself many times.

The woman said the girl had been left alone for just a couple minutes today and had found a way of removing the helmet. She'd grabbed the hammer from the family's toolbox, which they kept in the basement and hidden in the room, closing the door. She then beat herself to death.

During this explanation, my back up had called for detectives and began to collect identification from all the people present.

We were pretty sure this was a homicide; not what the family was trying to portray. Most likely, the killer was still in the house, acting like they, too, were grieving.

I continued to interview the woman and looked for anything in her behavior that didn't fit, anything in her explanation that didn't make sense.

I had learned by this time that confrontation during an interview was pointless; instead, I let the people talk themselves into a hole while I documented the inconsistencies of their claims.

Although her claims were bizarre, everything fit: the physical evidence, the girl's injuries, the weird grief, and the relief emotions of the family. It all fit.

The detective who was assigned to the case arrived, and immediately the whole scene changed.

The other detectives on the department referred to him as Colonel Flagg, naming him after the paranoid character on the TV show M.A.S.H. The similarities were pretty accurate.

Flagg, the character on M.A.S.H., saw conspiracies everywhere; so did Detective Flagg, who loved to make a simple scene dramatic.

He had us detain the entire household, then called for the shift supervisor and Lieutenant. He criticized us for not calling him sooner. We had been in the house seven minutes when we called for him.

He came in, took one look at the scene, and loudly proclaimed, "This is a homicide. She's been dead a long time, and her skin is marbled." (Blood pools when a person dies, causing the skin to have a marbled appearance.)

He looked at the splatters on the walls and said, "That's high-velocity splatter. No way this girl could have created it. She's too short; a large male did this blood splatter!"

I'd been on cases with him before, and he was very theatrical and loved to be the center of attention.

He said out loud that the girl's physical appearance proved that the family had been starving her and that they had most likely killed her as well.

The family was shocked, and they were instantly outraged. Any cooperation we were going to get from them was instantly gone.

Anyway, in short order the theatrical Detective Flagg had turned the quiet scene into a circus, and we were banished to the perimeter.

After several hours, the body was removed and we were released to write our reports.

Occasionally, family members would be ushered out by patrol units and taken to the station for interviews.

A couple days later, it was determined that the girl had, in fact, killed herself. Her mental illness was well documented, as were her repeated self-inflicted injuries.

I went to Flagg's office to ask about the case.

His demeanor had changed; he was now confidently telling me how he'd disproved the homicide theory and that he'd known immediately when he arrived that it wasn't a murder.

I listened to him closely while he rationalized the day.

In his mind, the scene had changed. We had called him to report the homicide, but when he arrived he knew immediately that this wasn't a homicide.

He described the family's behavior, the girl's wounds, and the damaged helmet. He chastised me for not knowing better.

He looked down his nose at me, peering over the reading glasses he kept perched there, his lips pursed.

I said, "You know, there's just one thing I'm not clear on..."

He said, "What's that?" sure that he could clear up the discrepancy in my lack of understanding of the evidence.

I said, "At the scene, I clearly remember you making the comment that the blood splatters were caused by a large male. I know I was amazed that you knew the person who killed the girl was not only large, but was male as well, and you knew all that from just the splatters on the wall?! How did you know that?"

We stared at each other for a long time and said nothing. (Colonel Flagg could never be wrong on the show *M.A.S.H.*, and neither could Detective Flagg.)

His face was getting redder and redder, veins poking out on his forehead.

I admit, I was smiling a huge (fuck you) smile. Finally, I had the arrogant dickhead trapped in his own bullshit!

He blew up and threw me out of his office.

I've always had a way of making friends and smoothing out the ruffles in relationships.

28 The Voices Made Me Do It

MARION COPE LIVED IN A rundown part of the city. It wasn't as bad a central city, but it was close.

The houses were all sixty years old or more, and they were built on the bed of an old river that had run through the middle of the city.

The river had changed course many years ago, and the land had been reclaimed and built up with houses, a community swimming pool, and an outdoor rodeo arena.

The area had been ravaged by gangs, and when meth hit the streets in the early 90s it was a knockout blow.

The area never recovered, the pool was closed, and the arena closed as well. Marion had been renting a house in the area.

He could afford the rent as long as he shared expenses with a roommate, so he had chosen to room with a friend he knew was in need of a place to stay.

His friend, Bill Williamson, had been kind of odd all through high school. They had stayed in touch through the years, and Marion never quite understood what bothered his friend. He knew that he had some kind of mental illness, but it seemed to be in check as long as he took his medication.

Marion didn't feel it was his place to ask about the illness. He believed that as long as he was fair to his friend, nothing bad would happen.

Bill Williamson never talked about the voices he heard. They would tell him things. Sometimes the voices were loud, sometimes a whisper. He would hear things, people walking past, voices, dogs barking. He would often turn to answer a question or reply to a comment and find there was no one there. The comments, questions, and whispers were all in his head. Usually, they were harmless comments; sometimes they weren't.

When he was on his medication, the voices became so quiet, often-times he'd barely realize they were there. Like a wisp of smoke appearing out of thin air across the room, he was never sure if they were really there or if they were his imagination.

One day, Williamson was walking back from the convenience store after buying some cigarettes. A neighbor had been dealing meth and offered Bill a small bit of the sandy, red-colored drug.

Mexican meth was red in color at the time. Each process of manufacturing meth creates a signature appearance. Sometimes it looks like little crystals of ice, sometimes yellow, sometimes red and brownish.

Bill was aware of meth and had never tried it. His doctors had given him medication that made the voices go away for the most part, but the medication made him feel fuzzy and he always felt like he was in a daze.

He asked the neighbor what the meth would do for him.

The dealer said the meth would make him as sharp as a razor and that things he had never understood before would become really clear.

Bill heard the magic words: "sharp as a razor."

That was what he wanted. To be clear, to think clearly, and to be able to function normally for once in his life.

He accepted the drug and went home to take it.

Bill was awake for three days straight the first time he took meth. He said he felt alive for the first time in his life. He had an amazing amount of energy, and his mind was racing, understanding things he'd never been able to before.

He felt he could fix anything. He took the television apart and was sure that he could find a way to make the phone work through the TV.

Finally, he came down and crashed.

Sleep came with a vengeance, and when he awoke he felt like shit. The dullness had returned.

He was exhausted. He had forgotten to take his medication during the three-day burst of energy the meth had given him, so he took a pill.

The voices were loud now, telling him over and over that the pills he was taking were poisoned and that Marion had tried to poison him.

He ignored the voices, and after a couple days of pills, they subsided into the background of his mind, back into the fog.

A week or more went by, and Bill was out for a walk. The meth dealer saw him and stopped him and offered more meth, twice as much as he had the past time they had met.

He told Bill he could stay "up" as long as he took the drug, and he never had to come down as long as he kept taking it.

Bill liked how sharp he felt on the drug, so he accepted it and asked where he could get more when he ran out.

The dealer told him to come and see him; he'd make sure Bill was given as much meth as he could afford. He told Bill the meth was a gift, but now he'd have to buy it. Bill agreed.

He took the meth, and the high returned; not as intense this time, though, so he doubled the amount he took.

The voices returned and explained that Marion was a demon and that if he watched closely, he'd see signs of him being a demon.

Bill did watch, and on the fifth day without sleep he thought he saw for a brief moment something in Marion's eyes. A creature was behind the eyes themselves!

He jumped back, frightened.

The voices were right! Marion was a demon, and he'd been trying to poison Bill.

Bill left the house and walked for a while, unsure of what to do. He hadn't taken his medication for some time, and the meth had his tormented mind racing.

The voices were like a chorus; he couldn't shut them out.

They demanded that he kill Marion.

He had to save himself from the demon before the demon killed him. He made up his mind to do just that and went home.

He attacked Marion immediately after walking through the door.

Marion put up a good fight, but he didn't realize that Bill intended to kill him. Bill beat him senseless, then stabbed him, wounding him severely.

The voices weren't satisfied that the demon was dead.

Bill picked up Marion's head and looked into his eyes, looking for the demon hiding inside. He saw the demon hiding in fear, lurking behind Marion's eyes, flitting back and forth, trying to find a place to hide; trying to find a way out and kill Bill.

The voices told Bill he had to find a way to kill the demon. Only then would he be truly safe.

Bill went to the garage just outside the house and picked up a piece of rebar. He returned to the house and knelt over Marion, then stabbed Marion in the neck with the rebar.

Blood sprayed all over him as he pulled the rebar through the opposite side of the neck, then began to twist.

Bill twisted Marion's head completely off.

He then looked into the eyes of the detached head, trying to see the demon.

It was gone. He was safe.

He pulled Marion's body into his bedroom and hid it underneath the mattress.

Bill put Marion's head in a small garbage can in the kitchen.

Finally satisfied, he went back to trying to make the television work, adding wires and removing circuits.

His mind was racing, sure that he could repair it and make the phone and the TV work as one.

The fears of the demon in his dead friend were gone; the voices were quiet.

We got the call when friends of Marion's came over to the house, looking for him. They saw the blood sprayed all over the carpet and walls, and television parts and wires all over the house.

They began to search the house.

They went into Marion's room, smelling the unmistakable odor of a decomposing body, and saw the huge lump in the mattress.

Pulling up the mattress, they found Marion's decapitated body. They were horrified and called the police.

We found Bill in the garage, asleep. He was covered in Marion's blood, and when we asked him what had happened, he mumbled something about a demon and voices.

He was exhausted from the toll of the meth high.

It took the detectives quite a while to piece together what had happened in the house and why.

Bill had filled in the missing pieces of why he had twisted off the head of his friend after he was back on his medication and could think somewhat clearly again.

He claimed the voices had been silent ever since he'd killed the demon in Marion.

29 New And Improved Isn't Always Such A Good Thing

I HAD BEEN WORKING CENTRAL city for some time and started to notice an influx of heroin into the city.

I contacted a guy I knew in the strike force that dealt with narcotics and asked if they'd noticed it as well. He told me that there was no such resurgence of the drug in the city.

According to this expert, I must have been seeing a one-time event. Heroin was a thing of the past; meth was the drug of choice on the street, and no one would be interested in heroin as long as meth was around.

I told him that I had seen several cases and that it looked like heroin was back with a vengeance.

He laughed and said, "That's why you're on the street and I'm in here, on the Narcotics strike force. We're the experts, and you're the patrolman."

I was done trying to talk to this dickhead. I went back out on patrol.

Two days later, I got a call of an overdose. I went to the apartment and arrived well before medical. I went to the door and knocked, and a frantic man answered the door.

He said that his girlfriend had scored some "H" and that they were going to shoot up. He'd fallen asleep, and when he woke up she'd already shot up the drug and was lying on the bed. She'd stopped breathing. He was frantically trying to revive her.

I asked him how long she'd been asleep. He said for maybe an hour.

I looked at the woman's skin, and it had marbled. The blood pooled in a dead body and made the skin have a weird, marbled appearance. I could see she had been down for some time, the needle still stuck in her arm.

I looked at the frantic boyfriend, and I could see that he wasn't prepared to give up. There was no bringing her back, but he wouldn't accept that just yet.

I said, "OK, pull her off of the bed. We have to have a hard surface to start CPR."

He did pull her off the bed, and I said, "I'll do the chest compressions. You'll do the breathing."

I showed him what to do, and we started. He forced about four breaths into her lungs, and then she aspirated the contents of her stomach into his mouth.

This is the reality of CPR you never see on the TV: you get a mouthful of puke because some of the air always goes into the stomach and pushes the contents up the throat.

He wasn't deterred. He kept at it, trying to breathe life back into her and spitting out the puke as it blew back into his mouth.

Medical eventually arrived, and they could see she was dead; however, once CPR is started they have to continue. They could see this was pointless and asked me what was up.

I told them the boyfriend wasn't ready to give up. I'd started the CPR for his benefit. He needed to at least try to bring her back.

After a few minutes, they took him aside and explained that she was gone. He agreed. As awful as it sounds, he could taste the reality of her death. He was very upset but kept repeating, "At least I tried...at least I did everything I could...at least I tried."

The boyfriend had told me that they had scored some Mexican heroin and that it was supposed to be the best there was on the street. They were told it would be the best high from heroin they'd ever had.

I asked him what was supposed to be different about the heroin.

A paramedic on the scene spoke up. He said that they'd been on several heroin overdoses in the past two weeks. The heroin that had hit the streets was 99% pure. That was why people were dying.

In the past, heroin had hit the streets 60% or maybe 50% pure. The users then cut it down even more, making it safe to inject. The new batch was assumed to be as impure as the old stuff. It wasn't. So when the users cut it down and injected it, they were injecting a lethal dose. There would be no surviving this high.

We were cleaning up the scene afterward, and the paramedic had removed his surgical gloves, the same ones we all wore on scenes like this. He had picked up a flashlight that was on the nightstand and offered it to me. He said to me, "Here's your flashlight, officer."

I told him that it wasn't mine. I had my flashlight in my back pocket. I asked the Fire Battalion commander if it was theirs. He said no, that they all had their flashlights.

The boyfriend was watching this conversation, still kind of in shock from seeing his dead girlfriend.

He said, "I think it might be ours."

At the same time, the paramedic commented on the sticky stuff coating the outside of the long, black steel flashlight. He was throwing it up in the air and catching it.

The boyfriend shook his head and said quietly, "Umm...ya... you might wanna put it down."

The paramedic said, "Why?"

The boyfriend replied that the flashlight was the dead woman's dildo. He said that she had used it often and had been using it before they bought the heroin a couple hours before.

The look on the paramedic's face was priceless. He didn't catch the flashlight again and let it drop to the floor. He began trying to sanitize his hands.

The entire fire crew erupted in laughter and wouldn't give him anything to clean off his hands. He ended up going into the bathroom and frantically washing his hands. Even the dead woman's boyfriend laughed.

The heroin that had hit the streets had been found over and over to be too pure for its users. The suppliers were killing off their customers by offering the new and improved heroin. Word would be out soon to be careful of the new product. There would be several dead heroin users in the next few weeks before the word made it out to everyone.

I made sure to forward every case involving a heroin overdose that I was involved with to the Narcotics strike force, making sure the brilliant agent I'd talked to received each copy. So much for being in touch with the streets.

30 Sometimes Things Got Out Of Hand

COPS WERE CONSTANTLY PLAYING PRANKS on each other.

Jim Handy and Kevin Larson were competitors in the department. They'd been in patrol together on the same squad, working the same shifts. They each had a wicked sense of humor.

The two cops were every Sergeant's nightmare.

They were constantly pushing the limits of what they could get away with, breaking rules they could get away with breaking, and bending the ones they couldn't.

One of the long-standing rules was that we couldn't leave the city to eat lunch.

After several years of eating at the same restaurants, the temptation to eat at a new restaurant outside of the city was too great for the two officers. They started to sneak out of the city at lunch and eat at a newly opened restaurant.

After they'd been going there a while, Jim got up to use the restroom and left without paying for his food, leaving Kevin to pay for the bill.

Jim laughed about it the next day in briefing, telling everyone that he'd stuck Kevin with the bill. Of course, the cops ridiculed Kevin for being so dumb and falling for the prank.

Kevin was plotting his payback.

He pretended that he was OK with the prank and continued to go to the restaurant. Jim would go with him, but he knew payback was coming; he just didn't know when or where it would be coming from.

One night, Kevin finally set Jim up. He went to the vehicle fleet manager and was able to get a copy of the key to Jim's patrol car. He had to pay the guy extra to make the key and explain what he planned to do with it. He agreed to return the vehicle key when the prank was over.

They went to eat as usual, but what Jim didn't know was that Kevin had told the dispatchers to give him a fake call about ten minutes into the meal.

Kevin received the call and went out after paying for his meal. Jim was comfortable now, relaxed that at least today nothing would happen.

Kevin left and picked up another cop. They drove back and took Jim's car from the parking lot of the restaurant. They drove it to the center of town and parked it in one of the busiest intersections.

The car was running, emergency lights, headlights, and warning flashers turned on, and the siren blaring. The doors were locked.

It took about two minutes for the Sergeant to find the vehicle and ask Jim over the radio why his car was parked in the intersection, lights and sirens blaring.

Jim ran out of the restaurant; his car was gone.

He had to explain why he was out of the city, and he had no explanation as to how his car had ended up in the city without him in it. Kevin was covered; he was on the fake call. Everyone heard it dispatched. But Jim knew what had happened. You'd think that they'd stop here…nope.

Kevin was married and had a really hot girlfriend on the side. He'd met at her at work, and he'd told her that he was single and that he could only see her occasionally because he had to work so much. He told her that he had to pay child support and picked up all the extra shifts that he could (he had no kids at the time), lying to cover his frequent absences when he was with his wife. The hot girlfriend believed him, and for a while he was able to cover his tracks with both women.

Jim thought this over and saw a way to one-up Kevin supremely.

Jim was talking one night about his new girlfriend. Jim was divorced and frequently dated different women. He was at Kevin's house and asked Kevin and his wife if they'd like to go out to eat with him and his new girlfriend. He said he felt that she really might be "the one", and he wanted them both to meet her. He raved on and on about her and convinced the couple to go out to eat with him and the new girlfriend.

Jim was sneaky as hell.

He'd talked to Kevin's secret woman on the side and told her about Kevin's wife. He agreed with her that Kevin was an asshole and a pig. He let her get herself really worked up and furious, adding in comments here and there about how Kevin had played her. He suggested that they play a prank on Kevin and pay him back in a way that he deserved. She agreed.

The night of the dinner date came, and Kevin and his wife arrived as they had planned. Jim made them wait, making sure they were seated and that Kevin had no escape. Then he walked in with Kevin's secret woman on the side.

He sat down and introduced Kevin's girlfriend to Kevin's wife, the two men eyeing each other, Jim smiling huge, Kevin seriously about to shit himself.

The two women talked about their men, and the hot girlfriend asked Kevin's wife how long they had been married. She explained that they'd been happily married for five years! They were thinking about having children but hadn't had any yet.

The girlfriend nodded; some day she wanted to have children, too, she just hadn't found the right man yet (glaring at Kevin).

Kevin's wife was unaware of the nonverbal communication going on and just kept chatting about their lives and how beautiful their wedding had been. The girlfriend decided to turn it up a notch or two.

She had arrived dressed to the max, and she'd turned on the heat, making Kevin squirm as much as possible. She started rubbing on Jim and kissing him, whispering how she couldn't wait to leave the restaurant and fuck his brains out; she whispered this just loud enough for Kevin and his wife to hear.

Kevin's wife was shocked. She was a churchgoing girl, prim and proper; the word 'fuck' had never left her mouth in public. She was disgusted and misinterpreted Kevin's obvious discomfort as the same disgust; it wasn't.

Kevin was forced to play the part, watching his best friend and his now ex-girlfriend rubbing and dry humping each other in the restaurant.

Eventually, they all left, Kevin and his wife in one car, and Jim and Kevin's now ex-girlfriend in the other. The hot girlfriend made sure that Kevin saw her rubbing Jim's dick with her hand in his pants pocket as they walked to the cars. Kevin was furious, but the night wasn't over yet.

A half an hour went by with Kevin listening to his prim and proper wife complaining about the slut that Jim was dating. She asked Kevin how Jim could possibly think that she was "the one?" Why couldn't Jim see what a slut she was? Kevin was silent.

Kevin and his wife arrived home, and the phone rang. Kevin raced to the phone, afraid to let his wife answer, afraid of what she might hear or be told. He said, "Hello?"

His girlfriend was on the other end, moaning and panting. She had called to let Kevin know that she was having sex with Jim and wanted him to hear it while it was happening. She and Jim passed the phone back and forth, commenting to Kevin about how great dinner was while they fucked and talked on the phone.

All Kevin could do was listen and fake the conversation, nodding and responding to their comments. He was afraid that if he hung up, they'd call back and his wife would answer; then who knows what she'd hear?

Jim won this battle big time. Kevin had nothing that could top this.

When Jim shared this in briefing one night, we all laughed so hard, we could hardly breathe.

Kevin had finally been humbled, and no one could believe the perfection of the prank. It was a thing of beauty in the Cop world.

31 Sending Out Positive Energy Makes All The Difference

LISA JUDKINS AND HER BOYFRIEND, Travis Meeke, were both adventurers.

They had met in California and had decided to go on a road trip to see the world. They had read many stories about people in the late 1960s and early 1970s traveling the country and living out under the stars. The both longed for what they felt was a simpler time: the 60s and 70s. They were raised near Berkeley and had heard the stories about the era all their lives.

The second week of their amazing trip to see the real world under all the technology and falseness of the modern world had them landing in the rail yards that ran through our city.

Lisa was a beautiful girl and immediately attracted attention in the homeless shelters they frequented. Travis was very proud of the woman he was with and that she had chosen him to be her man.

They were total misfits in the world of the homeless. Young, beautiful Lisa, and smiling, shiny Travis. So in love, they were unaware of the company they were keeping. They actually believed the hippie bullshit they'd been told about the world at Berkeley.

Travis told me that he thought that if they sent out positive energy to the world, the world would return it. They were friendly to everyone they met.

They had taken up residence in an abandoned railroad caboose in the rail yards and had stayed there several days, keeping a regular schedule. Eating meals at the homeless shelter, meeting people, and talking to everyone in this totally naïve and unaware state of mind. Many people had noticed them.

The third night after they ate, they said goodbye to everyone at the soup kitchen. They were leaving in the morning for whatever the road and the railways would bring them. Smiles on their faces, they waved goodbye and headed back to the caboose.

They had no weapons, they hadn't locked the door to the caboose, and they had nothing but their positive energy to defend them from the real world.

About an hour after they went to sleep, the caboose door opened, and in stepped a man.

He had an aggressive attitude and beat the shit out of Travis, forcing him out of the caboose. He then pulled a knife and began to rape Lisa at knifepoint. She screamed over and over for Travis to help her.

Travis was her boyfriend, but he was no defender. He was gone, he left her and went for help—or at least that's what he said later. He eventually did get help, but it was much later.

Lisa was raped by the unknown assailant many times, both anally and vaginally. He beat her repeatedly while he raped her. When he'd finally finished beating and raping her, he held her down.

She later told me that he said he wanted her to remember this night for the rest of her perfect fucking life. He took the knife and cut deep cuts in her beautiful face. The rapist then left the caboose.

She screamed for Travis, but he was long gone.

We searched the rail yards and homeless shelters for anyone who might have heard or seen anything. No one knew a thing. Everyone knew the pretty young couple we were asking about. Everyone had seen them. The list of possible homeless men mentally ill enough to pull of the rape was huge.

To make matters worse, Lisa and Travis never saw the rapist's face. The caboose was pitch dark. They could barely see anything from the huge ballpark-style lighting that illuminated the rail yards.

Lisa and Travis flew home to their parents a few days later, their world tour cut short by reality.

The people at Berkeley were full of wonderful, amazing stories about traveling the world in the 60s and 70s. The problem was, the people who told those stories were the lucky ones who had survived.

The bodies that ended up buried in deserts and fields all over the country had no such stories to tell. They'd faced the same reality that Lisa and Travis had. Their positive energy hadn't protected them.

32 You Reap What You Sow

ONE NIGHT, I WAS SENT to back up officer Divot on a fight at a hotel.

We arrived at the hotel, and Divot started doing what he called investigating. Basically, he belittled people until they either told him something or he got tired and just arrested them; this was his way of "investigating."

I arrived, and Divot asked me to keep one of the guys he had cuffed inside of my car while he interviewed the other.

I sat the guy inside of my car after Divot had searched him. He was handcuffed, and we sat there for some time, watching Divot talking shit to the other guy.

I started to talk to the suspect in my car. He said his name was Gary.

I asked Gary, "What happened here tonight? Why were the two men fighting?"

He wouldn't reply. He said they weren't fighting and he had no idea what I was talking about.

I told him, "Look, man, honesty goes a long ways with me. Tell me what happened, and maybe we can work shit out."

He was silent for a long time, then said, "Honestly?"

I replied, "Yes, honestly."

He said nothing for some time. I could tell he was really tired, exhausted more like it. Sweating profusely and tired.

It was cold outside, so his sweating told me he was most likely on something.

I just waited. Finally, the silence was too much, and he started to talk.

He said, "My name isn't Gary; it's Ronnie Bennett."

I nodded, remaining silent.

He said, "We, me and the other guy, were fighting over meth. I was gonna sell him some meth, and he tried to rip me off. I'm not gonna be ripped off by some fuckin' tweeker."

I said, "So do you know this other guy's name?"

He said no, that he just sold him "Ice", and that was it. They'd meet after the other guy called him, and he'd sell him some "Ice."

I said, "By 'Ice', you mean meth—the clear stuff?"

He said yes, that he wouldn't deal the dirty stuff that was on the street now. He had standards and wouldn't compromise by selling what he thought of as dirt.

This surprised me—a meth dealer with product standards—but I said nothing.

Divot had finished investigating and returned to my car. He asked me what I'd learned from my suspect.

I told him the guy's real name and that the fight had been over meth.

He said, "Is he carrying?"

I said, "You searched him; you tell me."

Divot blew up. Handling any call made him tense and edgy.

Personally, I think he was afraid that people would realize he had no idea what the fuck he was doing.

He was happiest polishing the brass, cleaning guns, and bragging about the latest SWAT call he'd been on. He did best in very structured environments. He fell apart in the chaos of the street. It was too chaotic and complex for his black-and-white thinking.

Anyway, Divot threw a few insults my way, then called my suspect a piece of shit, telling him that his meth problem would get him landed in jail tonight. He threatened Ronnie with being raped in the jail if he didn't start talking to me and stormed off.

I rolled up Ronnie's window and said, "Jesus, that guy's a dick."

Ronnie laughed; he agreed.

We were there a few more minutes, and finally I told Divot I'd take my guy to jail and get the paperwork started. He agreed, and I left the scene.

I arrived at the jail and asked Ronnie my standard question: "Are you carrying anything? Because once we're inside, if they find anything, you'll get charged; out here between me and you, it's another thing."

Ronnie looked at me, staring long and hard, then finally said, "He missed something when he searched me. I have some Ice on me now."

I said, "Where is it?"

He said, "It's in my shirt pocket."

I looked in his pocket, and there was a baggie sealed with about a gram of Ice in it. It was clear and looked just like small crystals of Ice.

I said, "Jesus! That's about the purest stuff I've ever seen."

He agreed.

I spoke to him for some time outside the jail about meth and the toll it was taking on his life. He was twenty-five years old and looked forty.

He was worn out. The life of dealing and using had beaten him down fast.

The more we talked, the more I could see he was hearing me. He started to cry, then really started sobbing.

I let him cry for some time until he gathered himself. He told me to keep the Ice, he wouldn't tell anyone.

I said, "What do you mean?"

He said he'd been stopped by cops several times and they'd taken his Ice for themselves.

I said, "Oh ya? Like who?"

He wouldn't tell me who, but his body language and eye contact had me wondering.

I told him I'd give him a break tonight. I'd throw the Ice away. I wanted no part of that shit.

I parked in front of a dumpster and made sure he watched me throw it away.

I took him into the jail and started the paperwork. When it came time for his charges, I only added what Divot had wanted him charged with: disorderly conduct.

He stared at me and said, "Why aren't you charging me with the drugs?"

I said, "I told you, honesty goes a long way with me. You were honest, so take this break and do something with it. Keep going the direction your headed, and you're gonna be dead before you're my age."

He stared at me in disbelief.

I told the correctional officers that Divot would be coming in for him and that these were the only charges he had.

Ronnie just stared at me quietly as they processed him. I told him to take care and left the jail, headed out to the next call.

Several months later, I was at the mall with my wife and our three little kids.

I didn't look the same out of uniform. I looked totally different; combing my hair different and wearing baggy clothes, people rarely recognized me.

I was walking along with my kids in front of me, their mother closer to them than I was.

I heard a voice say, "Officer Fortier?"

I turned, and there was Ronnie with two of his friends.

I checked my kids; they were still headed away from me. We were on the top floor of the mall. I started to slowly walk to the rail overlooking the bottom floor of the mall.

Ronnie reminded me of who he was while his friends walked on either side of me. Basically, I was surrounded.

No problem, as long as the kids kept going with their mom. They had no idea of this world; unfortunately, they were about to get a close up of what Dad did at work.

I walked to the rail so I had my back to something while Ronnie talked. I told him I remembered him, and he kept making small talk.

I didn't know what he wanted, but I'd made my plans already if he decided to fuck with me. I'd already checked, and none of them had weapons. No bulges in their clothing, nothing apparently hidden.

They were all about my size, so no one was a monster to fight. I sized them up, picking out which guy I'd go for first.

They were acting cocky, comfortable, self-assured, having me outnumbered three to one. That was a mistake.

Ronnie was about to go head first over the rail.

One guy had his hand in his pockets—he'd be next; he wasn't paying attention to me, and that would be his mistake.

The third guy was leaning over the rail, watching the girls below us. I figured he'd be the last I'd have to worry about; he might go over the rail as well.

Reality was, they were all tweekers.

I might end up hurt, but I'd fuck them up. I did this shit every night, outnumbered and overwhelmed.

While I was talking to Ronnie and planning his beat down, I heard my wife's voice say to my oldest son and daughter, "Go tell Daddy we're hungry and we want to eat."

A few moments later, I felt tiny hands wrapping around my legs, and I looked down to innocent little faces smiling at me.

"Daddy, we're hungry!" they said together.

I looked at Ronnie, and he smiled. "These are your kids?"

I told them to go now to their mother and pushed them off me.

Looking back now, I realize that my kids were never in any real danger. If Ronnie had wanted to jump me, he could have. He recognized me way before I saw him.

I started to casually close the distance between myself and Ronnie. I would have to hit first—and hit hard. No fucking way I'd let these guys touch my kids.

I started to close the distance, and he must have realized I was about to strike; he held up his hands and said, "Wooaah! Wait a minute, man—you misunderstand me!"

I stopped. Up on the balls of my feet, I was ready to fuck him and his homies up if they laid one finger on my kids.

Ronnie said, "Easy, man! Easy! I just wanted to thank you. I thought about what you said, about the meth and giving me a break. I had a lot of time to think in jail. I talked to several of the inmates in jail, and they knew you. They said you always treated them with respect, so I figured you were legit. I just wanted to say thanks, man. That's all."

He stared at me, smiling.

Still not convinced, I looked to make sure the kids were back with their mother. They were, but she still hadn't clued in to the body language.

Ronnie stuck out his hand and asked me to shake his.

He said, "Thanks!"

I shook his hand, waiting for the attack that never came, planning to break his arm first, then go to work on the other two.

Nothing happened; no attack.

He left the kids and me alone after thanking me over and over again for giving him a break.

Almost as an afterthought, he said, "You're good with me, man; your kids are safe! Have a good day, Slick."

I guess my state of mind must have at least been obvious to him.

It wasn't to my wife.

We sat down to eat, the adrenaline still flowing.

I wasn't hungry. She said, "So who were those nice boys you were talking to?"

I stared at her for a minute, dumbfounded, and said, "No one; just guys from work."

She said, "Well, they seemed nice."

I sat in disbelief, still trying to come back down from gearing up to fuck up Ronnie and his crew.

I never went to the mall again with my kids or their mother. She had no common sense for the world I worked in, and I couldn't jeopardize my kids by being there in a crowd of what she saw as "nice boys."

33 Be Careful When You Poke The Bear

ONE NIGHT, I WAS SENT to the Emergency Room to pick up a guy who had been arrested and had been injured in the arrest.

It happened often enough. People don't want to go to jail with a smile on their faces. Some fight back, literally, and in the battle for their freedom they get hurt. It doesn't have to be police brutality, although that definitely can happen when you have to fight night after night, call after call.

I arrived, expecting to find a guy that maybe had a cut or a scrape that would keep him from being booked into the jail.

I asked the nurses where the guy was that I'd been sent to pick up. They gave me an accusing look.

I was puzzled; usually, they were talking all kinds of shit, joking, talking trash to me, and making smart ass remarks.

They weren't friendly at all, not joking. They had a serious and critical attitude.

They said, "He's back there in Room 6. The doctor isn't done yet."

One of them said, "What the hell happened to him?"

I told them didn't know, that I was just sent to pick him up. I didn't know about anything that had happened.

They looked at me disapprovingly, then replied, "Uh huh, sure."

I thought to myself, *What the hell is wrong with them? Moody ass nurses!*

I lived with one; they were all crazy. I'd seen this disapproving look many times at home for no reason at all.

I shrugged my shoulders and went to the room, pulling back the curtain and being surprised at what I saw.

I found a guy about thirty-five being treated by a doctor and two nurses. He had a catheter in that was draining urine from his bladder. The urine wasn't the usual clear or yellow color; it was bright red with blood. The guy was crying and looked seriously hurt.

I watched for a minute and saw them checking his blood pressure and monitoring his heart rate. This couldn't be right; I must have entered the wrong room.

I pulled back the curtain and checked the room: yep, it was #6. I thought, *What the hell? This guy must be a DUI.*

He'd obviously been in a crash and had been seriously hurt. They'd patched him up enough to book him for the DUI, but I'd been sent to book him into jail for a burglary. This made no sense. They must have two people up here to go to jail, not just one.

I went back to the nurses' desk and told them I was here for someone else. This guy looked like he'd been in a car crash; I was here for the guy who had resisted arrest on the burglary.

They looked at me for a second, and no one said a thing. Then one of them stepped up and replied, "You don't know, do you?"

I said, "Know what?"

I didn't even hear anyone transported to the hospital. I was way too busy working the central city area to listen to the radio for every call that went on.

I said, "I was sent because I had a break in the calls, and you guys said he was ready."

This guy had obviously been in a car crash. He was pissing blood and still in shock. He was still shaking from the trauma.

The nurse who had spoken up motioned for me to follow her, and we walked back to Room #6.

She pulled back the curtain, and we went in. She handed me a large plastic bag and said, "These are his clothes. We double-bagged them. You'll wanna put them in your trunk because they're pretty rank."

I said, "OK"; that wasn't unusual.

DUIs frequently pissed their pants, and oftentimes they were so drunk they'd shit their pants.

Nothing yet to explain to me where the burglar was.

I set the bag down and said, "So where's my guy? This is a DUI, right?" The doctor stopped and stared at me.

He said "No, this is the guy your guys brought in to be treated."

I said, "What happened?" The doctor stared at me disapprovingly.

He said, "He'll be ready in a second, then you can take him. You'll have to leave the room while we clean him up and remove the catheter."

I was baffled.

The whole emergency room was acting weird, as if I'd just done something they really didn't like. I was in the ER every night and had never been treated like this before.

I stepped out of Room #6 and had had enough.

I said to the nearest nurse, "What the fuck is wrong with everyone tonight? Jesus Christ, you guys act like I'm your worst enemy."

She didn't reply.

I was fed up; I had to deal with this moody shit at home, and I had no patience for it at work.

I called the dispatcher on the phone and asked her who I was here to pick up, specifically the name of the person. I told her they were trying to get me to take a DUI to the jail, which I could do, but I wanted to make sure I took the right person.

She told me the suspect's name.

I looked on the board that the nurses wrote the patient's name and room number on to track the constant flow of emergencies through the Emergency Unit. The names matched.

The doctor pulled back the curtain and said, "He's ready when you are."

The suspect stood up on shaky legs. I picked up his double bagged shit and piss-soaked clothing and took a hold of his arm.

I had to walk him out of the Emergency Room carefully. He was shaking severely and still lightly crying and gasping for air. He'd been really traumatized. He looked like shit.

I sat him in my car, hands cuffed in front; cuffing them in the back was out of the question. He was hammered. I put the bag of clothes in the trunk and got in my car.

I started it up, then said, "OK, man, what the fuck happened to you?"

He said, "One of you guys beat my ass 'til I shit myself and pissed blood—that's what fucking happened!"

I was thinking, *Ya, sure;* I'd witnessed many incidents of street justice, and none came close to this. He seriously looked like he'd been in a bad car wreck.

I said, "So what caused this to happen that you were beat so severely?"

He said, "Nothing. I was just walking down the street, and this cop pulled up and beat my ass."

No way that had happened.

I listened to him sob and whimper all the way to the jail. I took him in, and they already had the paperwork for him filled out.

I asked who the arresting officer was. They told me Riley Wilson.

I was shocked.

Riley worked my area and was notoriously lazy. That he had made an arrest at all was hard to believe, but that he did anything like this was nearly impossible to believe.

I said, "Can I see the paperwork?"

They showed it to me, and I saw that it was in fact Riley Wilson.

I said, "Jesus, he arrested someone?"

The booking officer laughed and said, "Yeah we had to show him how to fill out the paperwork; he said it was a new form and he wasn't familiar with it."

I laughed because they'd changed the form two years earlier; that was how often Riley went to the jail.

I constantly talked shit to Riley. We'd worked the same area for an entire year and he'd been a ghost in the area. I'd hear him on the radio, but he never showed up to any of my calls.

Riley was an ex-pro football player. He was huge, but in my mind he was a paper tiger.

He was insanely polite. I mean that literally. It drove me insane. He was like an English butler in the body of Junior Seau or Ray Lewis. A monster with disturbingly polite manners.

We were polar opposites. I was 5'11" and 190 lb, and I swore like a crazy man. Riley was HUGE and wouldn't swear, regardless of the situation.

He also had the work ethic of a sloth.

He never moved fast anywhere. He drove me nuts. That he could have fired up and beat this guy 'til he shit himself and pissed blood was definitely physically possible, but not something I could begin to imagine.

I called Riley on the radio and asked him where he was; I had his paperwork from the jail, and his guy had been booked.

He politely answered that he was in the station and thanked me for completing his paperwork. (Totally unnecessary, but like I said, he was polite.)

I went to the station and met with Riley.

He was unusually quiet, and I could see that he was still shook up. I handed him the paperwork and asked what had happened on the call.

Forty-five minutes later, Riley finished his story; at the twenty-minute mark, I was regretting that I asked him.

His explanation was filled with polite discussion and sidebars that drove me fucking crazy.

Like I said, he was everything I couldn't stand and didn't want to be.

With all of his polite bullshit, he could make a five-minute story drag out for hours. I'll spare you his account and cut to the chase.

Riley said that he and a female officer were sent to a burglary in progress. The female officer had arrived first. (When it came to responding to a call, he ALWAYS took his sweet ass time.)

When she arrived, she found a guy leaving a business with a portable welder. She stopped him, and instantly he became abusive. He repeatedly called her a "bitch" and a "fat cunt", and that's what Riley heard when he finally arrived and got out of his car.

Riley told me that he asked the man nicely to apologize to the female officer. He was polite and always told me and everyone else that we should all be gentlemen when speaking to ladies. ("Ladies" being *any* woman we encountered.)

The guy told him to fuck off.

Riley again asked the man to apologize to the young lady, saying he'd only ask him this one last time.

Riley said the guy went off on a verbal barrage that included accusing Riley of getting blow jobs from the ugly bitch cop and ended with him refusing to apologize to "the ugly cunt."

Riley put his head down and said nothing more for a few seconds. He sighed.

I asked him what happened then.

He said, "I lost my temper, Kiddo. I really lost my temper!"

I said, "And?"

Riley said he remembered picking the guy up by his shoulders and slamming him down on the ground—hard—three times. Then he blacked out.

I laughed hard at this.

Prim, Proper, and Polite—that was Riley.

Trying to imagine him picking this guy up and slamming him down on the ground for mere verbal abuse was too much.

I couldn't stop laughing.

Riley wasn't amused.

He apologized to me, politely saying that his mother had raised him as a gentleman. He was taught to be polite and courteous always, no matter what the circumstances.

He'd lost his temper at hearing the female officer referred to with such disgusting, foul language.

I couldn't stop laughing.

I patted the polite giant on the shoulder and said, "I'm glad to know something fires you up, Riley. I'll be sure never to call a woman a 'cunt' in your presence."

He winched at just hearing the word. I couldn't believe it.

I guess we all get fired up over something. I would be in a murderous rage at the drop of a hat over children being abused in any way.

For Riley, the breakdown of manners in the presence of a "lady" was his breaking point. He had no ability to rein his rage in when that happened.

From that point on, I kept my distance from Riley.

I was always foul-mouthed at work, and I didn't want to get a painful lesson in manners and respect from the monster English butler.

34 Cops Lie

I WAS SITTING IN A parking lot one night, writing up a case report, parked backed up to the rear of the lot so that no one could walk up on me while I wrote.

I had a reserve officer with me, and I told him to keep a watch out while I wrote.

It was serious business; people sneaked up on cops all the time while they did reports, and ambushed them.

I was about halfway through the report when the dispatcher came over the radio, asking for anyone to clear from a call and respond to a fight in progress. It was two blocks away from where we were parked.

The caller said there had been a party at the address and that there were about seventy-five people present. There was fighting now, and people were leaving rapidly.

I looked at the reserve officer, and he looked at me. He smiled.

I said, "Ya, we're going. Tell them on the radio while I get this report put away."

We took off out of the parking lot, and just before we arrived at the scene the dispatcher came across the radio and said that they had reports that someone had been stabbed.

We arrived and pulled up across the street.

We got out, ready to scrap with whoever decided that they wanted to fight. Immediately, the crowd parted, and I saw a guy lying face up on the front lawn of the home.

A young woman ran up to me and said her boyfriend had been stabbed on the front porch, which had been the location of the party. She said he'd been stabbed in the back during a fight and had collapsed.

I saw that he was lying in the front yard now. There was one guy trying to do CPR on him while the crowd watched. Most were too drunk to understand what had happened or to help. I walked up and talked to the guy doing CPR.

He was doing it wrong.

He was very drunk and scared.

He was pushing on the chest in the wrong place and way too hard; he'd kill the guy if he didn't stop.

I told him to stop, and he refused.

I said, "You're doing it wrong. Stop, or I'll make you stop."

He ignored me.

I told the reserve officer to keep the crowd off me, then I grabbed the guy doing CPR by the shoulders. I pulled him back pretty hard and started to check the victim out. (The reserve would tell me later that I'd thrown the guy all the way across the yard; I guess I'd been rougher on him than I realized.)

The victim had a thready pulse, which came and went, and his pupils were blown completely. His heart was beating, but the blood wasn't making it to his brain, and he wasn't breathing.

I advised dispatch of his condition and started mouth to mouth.

Moments later, the paramedics arrived and took over. They grabbed him and rushed him to the hospital.

Later, after we'd finished at the scene, I went to the hospital to check on him.

They told me that the single knife wound had been perfectly placed and severed his aorta.

His heart had continued to beat and pumped the blood in his body into his abdomen and chest cavity. They'd done everything they could to save him. They even cracked his chest open to try manual heart massage and had discovered the severed aorta. He was only twenty years old.

At the scene, we contacted several witnesses and wrote down information on all the witnesses we could find.

We were able to locate names of the possible suspects right away and learned that the victim had started the fight.

He was a scrapper and had been looking for a particular guy he wanted to fight. When he confronted the guy he wanted to beat up on the front porch, they'd started to fight.

Another guy had come from behind and stabbed the victim in the back; one quick stab that just happened to be perfectly placed, severing the aorta.

It was an amazing stab wound that rarely occurred on the street.

We did our part, and detectives had the suspect arrested and in custody within hours. Months later, we went to court, and he was convicted.

The next night, I was back at work, sitting in the same lot, writing another case report.

Cops will try to tell you that this shit doesn't bother them. I tried to pretend that it didn't bother me. I didn't let it in until years later.

I ended up at a junkyard, looking for a car that had been seized in an arrest. An informant had called and said that the car was loaded up with cocaine.

I was sent to search the car with a drug dog and told to recover any drugs. The informant wasn't mine, and when I arrived with the dog we found no drugs at all. The dog didn't even act interested in the vehicle.

I went back to the office of the junkyard and told the secretary that we were done and had found nothing.

She said, "OK", then looked at me funny.

She said, "Are you Zach? Zach Fortier?"

I mumbled, "Shit, here we go."

I then said loudly, "Yes. Why do you ask?"

As I'd noticed she was wearing a wedding ring, I was sure she was gonna talk shit to me about arresting her or her husband. I wasn't about to take her shit.

She held up her hands and said, "Please relax. I'm not angry with you. You don't remember me; that's obvious—but I never had the chance to thank you."

I was kind of shocked; people rarely thanked us for anything.

In my work, the people that usually remembered your name hated you with a passion. It was a long-standing joke between cops that you hadn't done your job if someone on the call hadn't asked you for your name, how to spell it, and badge number.

Anyway, she started to recall the night of the stabbing.

She was the young woman who had come to me to tell me her boyfriend had been stabbed.

She went on and on about how she'd watched my face as I did the mouth to mouth on her boyfriend, wiping the blood off my face that came spraying out of his mouth as he exhaled, then kept going.

She told me she was there at the hospital when I came up to check on her boyfriend and found out he'd died; she'd watched my reaction.

She said she was there in court as I testified as to what had happened at the scene that night.

She told me that they had a daughter and that they'd planned on getting married.

I told her I didn't remember the event. I didn't want to discuss it with her now, but she wouldn't let it go.

She said, "I wanna thank you anyway. I told my daughter how you tried to save her daddy and that you did everything you could do."

I said, "Look, I don't remember this call; sorry. Are you sure you don't have me confused with someone else?"

She said, "No, absolutely not! I remember you. I'll always remember you. Thanks again, Officer."

I left, pulling out of the gravel parking lot fast.

I wasn't mentally prepared for this.

I drove around for a while, then I had to pull over. I started to cry.

Years later, there I was, pulled over and crying for this dead guy and his little girl growing up without her dad.

Cops will tell you this shit doesn't get to them. Cops lie.

35 Rainbird'n

ONE SUMMER NIGHT, I WAS sent to a report of a large group of people gathered in the street.

The caller said that they were fighting and yelling at one another and we needed to get there fast. We got these kinds of calls all night long.

Sometimes you arrived to a quiet street, not a dog barking, not an angry voice or a door slamming, nothing.

It made you wonder: were you about to be shot at by a sniper? Had a crime just occurred where you'd just been the moment the call came in, and this was a diversion to get you to leave? You never had an explanation. There was rarely closure on a call; you just kept moving.

Anyway, I arrived, and so did my back up. Finally, I had a back up I could trust. He was a wiley veteran and had just come out of the Narcotics unit, Rinaldo Reyes. He wasn't an idiot like Divot or a traffic ticket-crazed stat whore like Skidmark. He was a balanced cop, smart and experienced. He'd worked informants successfully and solved many cases. I liked him being in my area; we worked well together.

We arrived and found the street full of people. Instead of the usual silent echoes of our footsteps, we found fifteen to twenty people in full all-out combat. We called for more units and waded into the melee.

We separated several combatants and sent them running off into the night. We didn't care why they were fighting; we just wanted the fight stopped before someone was seriously injured.

In no time at all, we were in the thick of the battle, throwing people off each other, yelling at others to back off, and then it all stopped.

We were surrounded, and the fighting stopped; now we were about to be attacked. The enemies now had a common enemy: US. Both sides started in on us. We went back-to-back and pulled out the pepper spray.

The spray was new at the time and hadn't earned the reputation (or respect) on the street it deserved. We were both on the SWAT team and had to be sprayed to carry the stuff.

It was liquid pain in my mind. I used it very sparingly because I knew the incredible agony it caused. We warned the mob to keep back or we'd spray them.

They kept advancing, mocking us, telling us we were gonna get our asses beat for interrupting the fight. One guy said we needed to be taught a lesson not to interfere in the affairs of the street.

He said confidently, "I hope you fuckers have medical insurance – you're gonna need it!"

Reyes yelled over his shoulder to me, "Are you ready?"

I said, "Ya! Let's spray these fuckers!"

The mob rushed us, and we went "Rainbird" on their asses. ("Rainbird" being a sprinkler used to irrigate large areas of land.) Anyone that came close got a face full of liquid agony. They quickly had a reality check and decided that the ass kicking we were about to receive was suddenly not worth it.

In less than thirty seconds, there was no one left in the street but Reyes and me. The mob was dispersed, running , stumbling, coughing—just trying to get away.

We laughed, turning to face each other, relieved. We laughed as someone can only laugh who's just narrowly avoided a life-and-death battle. We were outnumbered and had been surrounded, and any back up was minutes away, not moments. Without the pepper spray, we would have been in deep shit.

We laughed and high-fived, canceling our back up units and clearing the call.

No one had been seriously injured, and the calls were continuing to come in all over the city. We had other fires to put out, other battles to fight.

Another night, another call with Reyes and me again.

We were sent to a report of a suicidal man on the north end of the city.

We coordinated our arrival and arrived at the same time from opposite directions, driving in blacked out, all lights off. We used our emergency brakes to stop the patrol cars and not turn on the brake lights.

Silently, we got out and pushed the door to the cars shut slowly.

We listened; we could hear a family fight and walked to the sounds. The address was the one we were sent to for the suicidal man.

We knocked on the door and tried to talk the man out of the house. He came to the door but wouldn't exit the home; his wife and kids were inside.

He talked with us for about fifteen minutes, and we were getting nowhere with him.

He had a large knife and wouldn't put it down. He wasn't being aggressive to us or to his family, so we were at a standoff. We had nothing to gain by forcing the issue.

Finally, the guy was getting tired of us; he wanted to make a spectacle of his death. He wanted to make the whole family see him die, imagining, I guess, that they'd miss him—and in death, he'd finally feel he mattered.

He tried to close the door, and we rushed him.

He stood in front of his wife and children and raised the knife high in the air, readying himself to plunge it into his abdomen.

We entered the house as he raised the knife high, and I shoved him to the side, jumping back barely clear as he swung the knife wildly, narrowly missing me.

Reyes pulled his gun and was preparing to shoot the guy.

I know this is really stupid, but I had this thing where I never wanted to leave kids on the scene with a memory of us doing harm to their parents unless it was absolutely necessary.

I took a lot of shit for it, and I took a lot of risks as well.

I didn't want his children to see us kill their father or for them to watch him kill himself.

He'd swung at me wildly and missed.

I'd been in a few fights with guys with knives by this time, and I knew he was at his weakest point: the knife fully extended to his right side, the momentum of his swing stopped.

I stepped in quickly and pinned the knife against his side, both my hands on his hand, slamming him against the wall.

Reyes couldn't shoot him now, and I couldn't disengage him either. We were locked in a wrestling match over the knife.

The kids were screaming, and the scene was a mess.

Reyes yelled out, "Pepper spray!" and I turned my head away from the guy. Reyes sprayed his face, but still he didn't release the knife. He was screaming in pain, and I was coughing as well, but the fight wasn't over.

Reyes grabbed us and threw us both to the ground. He then pried the guy's hands free and cuffed him.

We took him out of the house and had paramedics respond to treat him for the pepper spray exposure.

We later put him into a nearby ambulance that had arrived at the scene.

Reyes looked at me, pissed off, and a bit alarmed.

He said, "What in the fuck were you thinking?"

I told him how I felt about fucking people up in front of their kids.

He just stared at me.

He then said, "Dude, that was a ballsy thing to do! You could have easily been stabbed or killed."

I didn't know if he was impressed or thought I was really stupid; either way, it was done, and the kids never saw us kill their father or watched him kill himself.

36 Too Close To Home

I GOT A CALL ONE night of a suspicious circumstance in an older rundown apartment house in the middle of my area.

The house had been owned by one of the many slumlords who owned property in the city and lived somewhere else so they didn't have to face the shitty housing they owned.

They had property managers rent the places out and collect the rent from whoever ended up there, and they then reaped the benefits, cash, tax deductions, etc., of being a slum lord.

The anonymous caller had made a very vague reference to something not being right in the rear apartment of the building and hung up. I got the call because it was my area, and we were unusually NOT busy that night.

Normally, a call like this would have sat for hours 'til we were absolutely not busy. For some reason that night, the powers that be gave us a break, and we were all trolling like street sharks: windows down, idling slowly back and forth in our areas, waiting for the chaos to break loose.

I was edgy because I arrived at work ready for a frantically busy night, and nothing had happened. The calm was eerie, and it made me nervous.

We all talked about it at break, wondering what the hell was going on. The normal rhythms of the street were off; nothing felt right. The city was quiet and calm. Most definitely not the norm.

I arrived at the address and quietly got out of the car.

I pressed the door closed on the patrol car until I heard it click softly, then slowly headed up the driveway to the rear apartment of the house.

It was pitch black, and the calm was creepy; not a sound. No dogs barking, no sirens from cops rolling from call to call, no gunshots…nothing.

I walked up the far side of the driveway, pressed against the next-door neighbor's house, taking three to four steps and stopping to listen. Nothing.

By this point in my career, I'd been ambushed several times. I never believed anything I was told about a call. I never took them at face value.

New cops will get pissed off at the dispatcher for not giving them every detail of the call, older cops know better than to listen to what the dispatcher tells them.

After I was reasonably sure no one was going to ambush me, I made my way to the door of the rear apartment. I listened outside the door for a few minutes to see if I could hear what was going on inside the apartment.

I could hear a soft banging inside, repeating randomly, and a baby screaming.

I was getting ready to knock on the door and noticed that there was no doorknob; just a rag plugged in the hole to keep the wind out and keep people from peering inside.

I slowly pushed the door open to the apartment and looked inside.

The apartment was actually a very unfinished back porch of the main house. It had a gas stove that had all the burners on, flames as high as they could be. I assumed they used the stove to heat the house.

There was a sink nearby that had water running heavily from a facet that was turned off. A bathroom built into what had been a closet with a toilet. There was also running water into an incredibly filthy tub.

There were three rooms total. The main living area, the "kitchen", and the "bathroom."

The banging noise I heard was an infant that was in the house… alone.

The infant was a little girl who had been left in the home. She was in a walker and was screaming, terrified and wearing only a diaper. She was the sole occupant of the apartment when I arrived.

I checked the place three times, looking for anyone. No one was there.

I couldn't believe that anyone would leave a young child alone in this place, open flames on the stove, running water in the sink.

The walls were roughed in, meaning they had no drywall or wallboard. Just 2x4s, exposed wiring to the lights, and an occasional plug. The ceiling was plywood, and a single wire hung down in the middle of each room: a light bulb hanging down from a utility outlet.

It was bare bones. More like what you'd see in an older rundown barn, not an apartment where a child would live—much less be left alone.

I called dispatch and asked when the call had come in. They replied that they'd held it an hour, nervous to send me on it if the city suddenly fell back into what we accepted as "normal." So I assumed the child had been left for an hour at least. Someone had come by and heard her inside crying and called.

I looked around and saw drug paraphernalia on the floors, a couple crack pipes and a syringe. I tried to calm the baby after I called for Child Welfare workers to come and take the child out of this shithole.

I waited an hour for them to show up. They finally did and weren't impressed with the home.

The child had finally calmed down a little bit. She was obviously very traumatized by being left alone for so long.

As we were getting ready to leave, the door burst open and a woman came running in.

I had my gun drawn immediately, expecting the attack to finally come. She was screaming at us, wanting to know "what the fuck are you doing in my apartment?"

She tried to take the baby from the Child Welfare worker, but I shoved her aside.

I asked her a few questions: was she the child's mother? Where had she been the past two and a half hours?

She spewed out "fuck you's" and "get the fuck out of my house!"

I don't remember what I did next.

My vision blurred, I had a wicked adrenaline dump, and then I started to hear and see again. The vision slowly came back into my eyes and sounds from the apartment started to come back; muffled, but I was aware of them.

I saw that I had the woman by the throat and the barrel of my gun under her chin.

I was talking to her and slowly started to be aware of what I was saying. I was telling her, "I should blow your fuckin' brains out right here, you glass dick-sucking bitch. I can smell the shit on you right now; you smell like piss. You've been getting high—you left your baby to get high! You don't deserve to have this baby, you piece of shit. I should do her a favor and put a bullet in your fuckin' head right now; she'd never remember you!"

She was quiet now, realizing perhaps that I wasn't the "Officer Friendly" she'd been told about in elementary school.

I was fucked up and damaged, and this call hit too close to home.

I held her there for a minute, her gagging from my grip on her throat. We exchanged a long, hard stare.

She started to cry and said, "I just want my baby."

I heard the baby cry, and then the caseworker said, "Jesus Christ!"

I gradually came back to earth and let her go.

The caseworker handed her the child.

I holstered my gun and gathered myself.

I started to write down her information and prepared to write the report.

The caseworker told me that they couldn't take the child from the home. I already knew this was going to be the case when the mother arrived.

The people who work these cases have very strict guidelines they have to follow. Common sense goes out the window, and children are seen as property of the parents.

If this were a disabled adult, the mother would have been arrested and the adult placed in a home; because it was a child, they released her to the mother.

These rules have since changed, but many children died because of the faulty "guidelines."

Before I left, I made sure the woman understood that I'd be watching her apartment. I'd be her worst fucking enemy. If anything happened to her daughter, she'd better pray I didn't get the call. Did she understand what I was saying?

She said yes, she understood, and nodded enthusiastically.

The caseworker stared at me, watching as I had the conversation.

I left the mother and the caseworker to work out their arrangements for their follow up and went to my car.

I hung around and waited for the caseworker to come out safely.

She came up to my car and said, "Are you OK?"

I said, "Ya, sure; another day in central city. How about you? Are you OK?"

She said, "Of course I am."

I said, "Ya well, hope we aren't back here in two weeks for another dead baby."

She said, "What do you mean, another dead baby?"

I told her I'd gone on the last three babies that had been killed in my area.

Kids die all the time in the central city; they get brutally shaken until their brains are so scrambled, they die from brain damage.

I'd been on one case a few weeks earlier where the child had been boiled to death in a pot of boiling water for peeing the bed.

My personal favorite (this really drove me into a rage): I told her I went to a class on child abuse and child homicide.

We were shown photos of a 2-year-old boy that had wet the bed. His loving parents had decided that he wasn't taking their discipline seriously enough. So the mother held him while the father (and I use those terms loosely) grabbed a Bic lighter and took hold of the boy's penis, stretching it away from his body.

The father lit the lighter and burned off the little boy's penis while his loving mother watched, restraining him and preventing his escape.

Was I OK? Fuck no, I wasn't OK.

I returned to the apartment the next week.

I meant to ensure that the child would survive this bitch who called herself its mother and not end up like the rest of the kids in these situations.

The apartment was vacant, emptied of all their stuff.

I asked all the neighbors where they'd gone. No one knew.

One guy finally admitted to me that he'd been the one that had called the week before. He said that the woman left in a hurry with the baby the morning after I came to the house.

He said she'd leave the child for hours at a time every night while she went out and got high, and he couldn't take it anymore. He was afraid that the child was going to get hurt or worse.

I asked him to let me know if he heard where the woman and her child ended up. I gave him my card and left.

I never heard from him, and I never saw the woman or the little girl again.

A SPECIAL PREVIEW OF

HERO to ZERO

ZACH FORTIER

Hero To Zero Preview—
Robert Suggs

I WAS WORKING AS A Military cop during the 1980s. It was a time of Nuclear Protests and people were nowhere near as pro-military as they are today. People hated you instantly if you were in the military. To be a military cop was the lowest of lows, the bottom of the military shit pile. This was where I met Robert Suggs.

He was a military cop, as I was, but much different from the rest of us. He embraced the "cop lifestyle" with a passion that was somehow intoxicating. He had a passion for being a cop that was unheard of in the environment of the military. Everyone else who wore the uniform looked down on us. But Suggs brushed all the criticism aside and looked upon being a cop as a calling; A worthwhile pursuit. He saw it as something to devote your life to and never feel ashamed of. His passion was feverish.

He not only worked as a military cop, sometimes sixty hours or more a week (we all worked long, long hours due to manning being at bare minimums), he also volunteered as a reserve police officer for the

Spokane Police Department. He lived breathed and ate COP, 24 hours a day 7 days a week.

I started to talk to Suggs on night shift when our patrols would overlap. I made no secret that I wanted to learn what he had learned from the Spokane cops. The military tactics were old and out of touch, we all knew that. Talking to Suggs was like jumping ahead twenty years in tactics, techniques and in the mindset that we were taught as MPs. He started to mentor me when he realized that I really was interested in the newer cutting edge tactics being taught on the streets of Spokane.

He tested the waters with me one night to see how committed I was to learning the newer stuff. He called for a meeting over the radio and I met him in a parking lot. He had another cop met us there as well. The other guy was newer, like me, and Suggs had been working with him as well; teaching him, undoing the mind set the military had instilled in him.

Suggs asked me how comfortable I was in the military's standard searches. Did I think that I could find a gun or knife and still keep my suspect under control? Ya, I did. I was pretty physically fit and cocky. I thought there was no way a suspect could get the best of me, search or not. I worked out constantly…it was a life long obsession. I told him I was pretty good at searching. He smiled, and I knew I had just made a mistake.

He laid out the scenario for me. A guy had broken through the gates of the installation, and was trying to access the nuclear loaded aircraft area. I had stopped and removed him from the vehicle and now had to search him. He took out the normally tedious and long-winded process of removing the suspect from the vehicle and took me straight to the search. This was a to be a test of my toughness and real desire to learn (as I was about to find out.).

I started out searching the "suspect" and as soon as I found the weapon it went to shit. He had told the other cop to fight like his life depended on it as soon as I found the weapon.

The fight was on. This was not similar to the military training I'd had become accustomed to. This guy turned on me and was seriously kicking my ass. There was no time out. It was a no holds barred, fifteen minute dog fight. Toward the end of the fight we were both bloodied up pretty good. Uniforms were torn and our normally highly polished boots were shredded. Neither one of us could defeat the other.

The idea of searching and containing the suspect was gone. I was raging mad and so was the "suspect". Suggs watched us fight and was talking shit to me the entire time, telling me I was loosing and that I was going to die. He said, "I thought you wanted to be a cop, this is a sad excuse for police work, you have let your suspect kick your ass". He kept talking shit to me until I was finally able to get the guy into an arm bar and nearly broke his arm. I was taunting him yelling, "Now what? Now what?"

Then Suggs stopped the fight. He separated us, standing between us, keeping us at arm's length. For us the fight was not over. This had gone way beyond training. Suggs laughed at us and told the other guy to go to his car. He left, staring at me the entire time. "Mad dogging" we would later call it on the street.

He said, "OK I see that you are serious and want to learn. First thing that you need to learn is you can never take for granted that you are gonna make it home. You survive the night by being meaner, tougher and most importantly–smarter than the other guy. You get cocky like you were tonight and you're gonna get killed".

He said that was the most important thing he learned from Spokane's cops. He said they did the same thing to him. They had him search a "suspect" and then it went to shit. He had to fight until he too overcame his "suspect". They told him 75% of the cops that came to their academy failed this test and were washed out. He said, "Congratulations you just passed their first test."

The next several months were meetings like this one. Not as violent, but they were as challenging. Suggs brought a concept to teach, an idea or a technique I had to learn, practice and master. He taught me a lot. Most importantly he taught me to always challenge what I was being taught. How to make it work for me on the streets or to get rid of it. He changed my mentality from what the military taught about following the rules and conforming to what they taught, to what carried me through my entire career. Challenge everything: every technique, every theory, and every tactic. Right or wrong he shaped the way I saw police work from then on.

Several months later Suggs was slated to get out of the military. His enlistment was up. I thought he'd surely be picked up by the Spokane Police Department. He told me as he left that he had tested for the police department and had scored well, ranking #1 on their list. He was confident he'd be hired. I never learned what happened after that. Later on, I heard that they did not pick him up, and that he had failed the psychological exam, but that was a rumor, and I never knew for sure. It was hard for me to believe.

As an MP, he was head and shoulders above the rest of us. He was an expert marksman, fit, and took the job to another level. He was very professional in the way he dressed and acted. He studied regulations and laws, and as I said, he worked as a reserve for Spokane police department.

Fast forward; several years have passed and I too have left the military police corps. I'm working for the sheriff's department back home, in St. Paul's. I was fortunate to be picked up by the sheriff's department at a time when hundreds of people were testing for only one or two job openings.

One night I was writing a report of an aggravated assault I'd been investigating. The patrons of a local truck stop had erupted into a knife fight, two men were fighting over a woman; one was her husband the other her boyfriend. The husband stabbed the boyfriend and the woman called the cops. We investigated the incident and I'd returned to the office to write my report.

I was sitting at a table we all used to write reports. We wrote them by hand then. PCs were a couple of years away from being practical. I took a break from writing, stretching my hands and looking around the room at the wanted posters hanging on the wall. Suggs had taught me well and I always kept up on the latest twix, teletypes, and wanted photos that were made available. The other deputies called me paranoid (not for the first time or the last time in my career).

One of the posters caught my eye. The guy looked really familiar. He was wanted by the FBI. I looked at him and tried to place him in my memory…I couldn't remember where I had last seen him. The name listed the wanted man as his Robert Michael Allen. The name did not ring any bells, but then as now…I never forget a face. The face for me is a lock; once I know your face I'll never forget you. Yet, I still can't remember names as easily.

At first, I was puzzled. I knew this face but from where? The name was totally unfamiliar to me. I read the poster and it said Allen had murdered a movie producer, the producer's father, and son. They'd been involved in a business deal and had stolen a couple of hundred thousand dollars from Allen. When Allen had discovered the theft he was furious and killed them, shooting them all. The wanted poster listed Allen as a "bodyguard" by profession, who was an expert marksman, and an avid gambler. He was considered armed and very dangerous.

I kept looking at the face. Somewhere I knew I had met this guy. At first I accused the other guys in the office of playing a prank on me and making up a fake wanted poster, and posting a picture of someone I knew as the bad guy. It made sense; we were always playing pranks on each other to break up the tension we all felt They all looked at me like I was crazy. The Sergeant told me to quit "being an attention whore and get back to your report". I ignored him. I knew that I knew this face.

The poster detailed a few facts about Allen, his height and weight, eye color, scars. He had a bullet wound on the big toe of one foot and several aliases. Reading the aliases I was stunned. Robert Michael Allen was his given legal name. He used several aliases, one of them was Michael Allen Suggs. The FBI now wanted the same "Suggs" that had mentored me years earlier in the military, for a triple homicide in Culver City, California. He was on the run, armed, and dangerous.

The light finally came on. I pulled the poster off of the wall and said "Holy shit I know this guy!"

The sergeant replied "Ya, ya sure you do we all know someone wanted by the FBI".

"No really I know this guy, I was in the military with him. He was a cop then and mentored me".

The Sergeant said, "That explains a lot! You were mentored by a murderer. Lemme see the fucking poster".

I handed it to him. "It says here to call the FBI if you have any information about him. Maybe you should call them deputy".

He smirked and looked at the other deputies in the room, and they all started laughing. They thought I was full of shit. I watched this room full of rednecks laughing and giggling about how they were making a fool out of the city boy. None of them had ever left the county they were born in. None had ever worked a murder, or even knew a murderer. I had grown up in the city. I saw my first murder at six years of age. It happened across the street from our house. I knew several of the local hardcore criminals from the time we were all little kids and growing up on the same streets. This bugged the hell out of my co-workers.

I thought it over and said "Ya, you're right I should call. Can I use the phone on your desk?" The room went silent.

"Sure, go ahead, knock yourself out". I picked up the phone and started to dial the number. The Sergeant hung up the phone and glared at me. He redialed the number from the poster and handed the phone to me. This was un-real.

The FBI answered the phone and I told them what I knew about "Suggs". The agent I spoke to was condescending as hell and said that "Suggs" was a killer and that they would find him. I told them he was well trained and had been a reserve officer for Spokane Police department. This was not on the wanted poster. Suddenly he too took me seriously. He asked my name, and spent the next forty-five minutes picking my brain about "Suggs". He then asked where I worked and if he could reach me if anything came up? I said "Sure". The room was still silent. The Sergeant who was so sarcastic was now silent and blankly staring at me. It was a snap shot of what my entire career would be like. An outsider, walking the line between cops and killers. Fitting in with neither.

I kept track of "Suggs" from that point on. About a year later I learned his body and his girlfriend's body were found in the desert. Apparently his girlfriend had been trying to break up with him at the same time he had been ripped off by the movie producer. "Suggs" kidnapped her and later killed her as well. I made a point of telling my arrogant Sergeant about Suggs' 4th murder and his apparent suicide. He had no comment.

This story is an excellent example of what later became a very common and amazing scenario with the cops I worked with and around. The "Hero to Zero" syndrome. Every single one of the cops listed in this book was outstanding in their own way. Every single one went from being considered outstanding cops and respected by their peers to being criminals, publically humiliated or at the very least no longer cops. They were handed their walking papers, and asked not to return. If there is any common denominator in them it is that they identified strongly with being a cop.

You can read about "Suggs" on the web. Google search "Robert Michael Allen" he is listed as #434 on the FBI's most wanted list. He was a good cop when I knew him and he was also later a multiple murderer. He is the only cop I will list by their real name here. The rest of the stories related here are also true, the names of the people involved have been changed. The cops were real cops, each outstanding in their own way. Somehow they all went down in flames, from *Hero to Zero*.

ZACH FORTIER WAS A POLICE officer for over 30 years specializing in K-9, SWAT, gang, domestic violence, and sex crimes as an investigator. He has written three books about police work. The first book, *CurbChek*, is a case-by-case account of the streets as he worked them from the start of his career. The second book, *Street Creds*, details the time he spent in a gang task force and the cases that occurred. The third book, *CurbChek Reload*, is by far the most gritty. The author is dangerously damaged, suffering from post-traumatic stress syndrome (PTSD) and the day-to-day violence of working the street. *Hero To Zero*, his fourth book, details the incredibly talented cops that he worked with but ended up going down in flames. Some ended up in prison and one on the FBI's ten most wanted list.

If you are looking for gritty, true crime stories, be sure to check out all of Zach Fortier's novels.

GET YOUR COPY OF
THE AWARD-WINNING AMAZON BESTSELLER
THAT STARTED IT ALL!

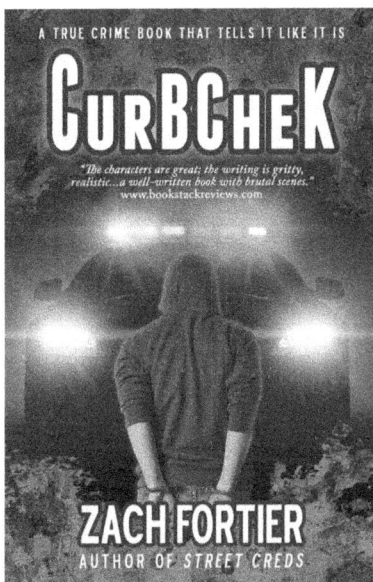

www.ingramcontent.com/pod-product-compliance
Lightning Source LLC
Chambersburg PA
CBHW021926040426
42448CB00008B/936